50 BEST
CYCLE RIDES
IN
CHESHIRE

Edited by Graham Beech

Published by Sigma Leisure – an imprint of
Sigma Press, 5 Alton Road, Wilmslow, Cheshire SK9 5DY, England.

British Library Cataloguing in Publication Data
A CIP record for this book is available from the British Library.

ISBN: 1-85058-348-X

Typesetting and Design by: Sigma Press, Wilmslow, Cheshire.

Cover design: Martin Mills

Maps: Orbit Design

Photographs: Graham Beech, except where stated

Printed by: Ashford Colour Press Ltd

Disclaimer: the information in this book is given in good faith and is believed to be correct at the time of publication. No responsibility is accepted by either the author or publisher for errors or omissions, or for any loss or injury howsoever caused. Only you can judge your own fitness, competence and experience. Do not rely solely on sketch maps for navigation: we strongly recommend the use of appropriate Ordnance Survey (or equivalent) maps.

Note on cycle hire: many cycle hire centres have closed over the past few years. Check in Yellow Pages for current hirers.

PREFACE

During 1992, I decided that Sigma really ought to publish a definitive guide to cycling in Cheshire, alongside our other books of cycle rides in the Peak District and the Cotswolds. For one person to write a complete book would have been a mammoth task, so I set about organising a small team to research, ride and describe 50 of the "best" bike rides. What you see is the result.

My role was to co-ordinate the exercise and to edit the descriptions into a reasonably-standard style. I also devised and tested some of the rides myself, to enter into the spirit of things.

In a first edition of a book of this sort, there are bound to be small problems and queries, but hopefully they will not detract from the pleasures of these rides. Any possible inaccuracies have been minimised by the kind and generous help of David Kitching, Countryside Manager for East Cheshire Ranger Service and his colleagues. When David offered to check out the rides, I imagined that he would just consult some definitive map on his wall. Instead, he despatched his own staff to get on their bikes and check out the rides "for real". That's dedication!

Many thanks also to my team of David Crewe, John Crewe, Jonathan Fox, James Harris, Philip Hobden and Matthew Irwin – and especially Sarah Cutler, an enthusiastic cyclist with many years of experience that proved invaluable in the planning of "50 Best Cycle Rides in Cheshire".

Graham Beech

WHO DID WHAT?

Our eight-strong team completed up to 13 rides each to produce "50 Best Cycle Rides in Cheshire". These are the credits (the numbers of the rides are in brackets):

Graham Beech: Bollington (8), Chelford (11), Macclesfield (34), Wilmslow (47), Wilmslow (48).

David Crewe: Bollington (7), Poynton (41), Styal (44).

John Crewe: Crewe (20), Sandbach (43).

Sarah Cutler: Alderley Edge (2), Alderley Edge (3), Congleton (15), Congleton (16), Macclesfield (36).

Jonathan Fox: Bollington (9), Chester (12), Chester (13), Crewe (19), Crewe (22), Disley (24), Knutsford (29), Lymm (31), Nantwich (37), Northwich (39), Warrington (46), Winsford (49), Winsford (50).

James Harris: Alsager (4), Congleton (17), Crewe (18), Crewe (21), Nantwich (38), Northwich (40), Tattenhall (45).

Philip Hobden: Chelford (10), Chester (14), Goostrey (26), Knutsford (28), Knutsford (30).

Matthew Irwin: Adlington (1), Ashley (5), Beeston (6), Cuddington (23), Disley (25), Holmes Chapel (27), Lymm (32), Macclesfield (33), Macclesfield (35). Prestbury (42).

Dave Edwards drew the maps, **Martin Mills** designed the cover, and **Annie Eastwood** word-processed most of the words. Our PCs got the words onto the pages and Manchester Free Press printed the books in record time!

CONTENTS

RIDES, RIDES . . .

. . . AND EVEN MORE RIDES!

Location Map

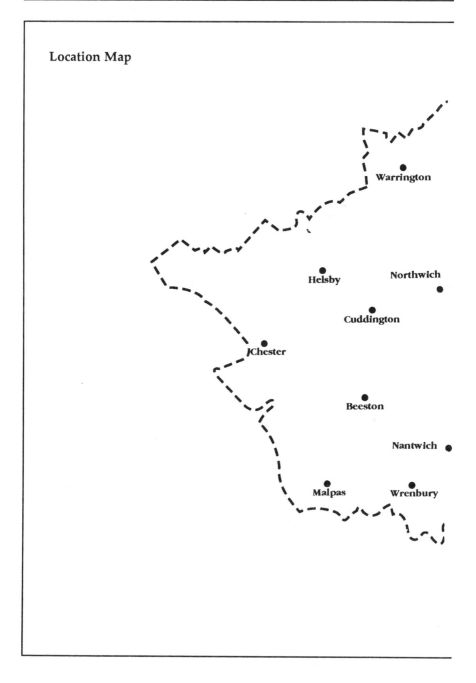

Setting Off! – rides 24 and 25, from Fountain Square, Disley

About this Book . . .

To the best of our knowledge, this is the first book to offer a selection of cycle rides covering just about all of Cheshire. Naturally, it can't cover every nook and cranny, but if you're a visitor, there's more than enough here to keep you occupied for a couple of weeks. And, if you're lucky enough to live in the county, you'll be surprised at how much you discover without the encumbrance of a car: you travel just fast enough to cover the ground in a reasonable time, and just slowly enough to take it all in. And, of course, there's always the attraction of "off-road" cycling where no car can go – and, no, you don't need a mountain bike (although you'll find it more comfortable on the bumpier routes).

County-wide coverage

The rides in this book are distributed reasonably equally across the north, south, east and west of the county. The starting points are arranged alphabetically so that you can easily select the rides that you want to try. You will find that there is always a good range of rides to suit all abilities, from a short ride taking a couple of hours on a shopper to challenging rides more suitable for enthusiasts with mountain bikes. Mostly, an average 'tourer' type of bike will be suitable.

Quiet roads and bridleways

As far as possible, busy main roads have been avoided, but – especially for longer rides – this is not always possible. Therefore, if you have inexperienced cyclists in your group, check the route description before you begin. The term 'bridleway' covers anything from a well-surfaced tarmac track to a bumpy, muddy path across open country. Again, read the route descriptions and decide if you and your bike are up to it. There are relatively few bridleways in Cheshire (and even fewer that the average cyclist can tackle) but they do exist and they make an interesting change from road riding. Since they are almost always in pleasant countryside, they are ideal for picnic stops away from fumes and traffic.

Note that *public footpaths* can only be used by pedestrians unless you, as a cyclist, have the express permission of the landowner – so avoid confrontation and possible legal action by only going where you are allowed.

Having said that, not all bridleways are properly signed – or signed at all (a few are incorrectly-signposted as public footpaths) so you will have to take our word that the ones described here are correct or, if you are planning your own rides, check a current Ordnance Survey map.

Cycling in Cheshire

Those of us who live in Cheshire are exceptionally fortunate: there are excellent road, rail and air communications to just about anywhere; most of us live within easy reach of such major towns and cities as Chester, Macclesfield and Manchester, but it's just as convenient to visit Cheshire's quiet villages or to amble along country lanes and by-ways.

But, best of all, Cheshire has such a wide diversity of countryside that makes it so appealing to walkers, cyclists, and all those who enjoy the great outdoors. Much of the centre of Cheshire is gently undulating – ideally suited to easy cycling with the family or to a long day when you can just eat up the miles. Elsewhere, and particularly in the east as you approach the Peak District foothills, there's no shortage of hills with superb views over the rolling countryside, with Cheshire's very own landmarks such as Beeston Castle or Jodrell Bank radio telescope visible for miles around.

The County Council is supportive of cycling, both as general recreation and as a tourist activity. In the late 1980s, a Cheshire Cycleway scheme was established with a booklet of rides and waymarking – you'll often see the blue signs as you cycle around Cheshire. Local Tourist Information Centres should keep up-to-date details on bike-hire

Cyclists and The County Council
Cheshire County Council is responsible as Highway Authority for the management of rights of way throughout the county. The Public Rights of Way Unit and Countryside Management Service are continually improving access and signposting of rights of way and would welcome any comments or queries regarding the off-road routes shown in this book. Please contact the Public Rights of Way Unit, Cheshire County Council, Commerce House, Hunter Street, Chester, CH1 2QP; Telephone: 01244 603265, or any Cheshire Information Point.

centres and other information for cyclists, so do contact
them if you can't find what
you want in this book.

Near to towns and public transport

Almost all of the rides start
from a town or reasonable-
sized village. There are two
reasons for this: if you don't
have a car (or don't wish to
use it), Cheshire's public
transport will get you there.
And, having got there, you'll
always be able to stock up with provisions.

Information for Cyclists

There are several magazines aimed at cyclists,
including *New Cyclist* and *Cycle Touring* where
you can read about the latest equipment, cycling
holidays and general information.

The largest organisation for cyclists is the
Cyclists' Touring Club (CTC), based at 69
Meadrow, Godalming, Surrey GU7 3HS; tel:
01483-417217. Membership is modestly priced,
with benefits that include an excellent
information service, organised tours and
holidays.

The British Tourist Authority publishes a booklet
'Britain - Cycling' *for overseas visitors only.*
This is updated every 2 years and can be
obtained from the BTA office in Regent Street,
London or overseas tourism offices.

Naturally, you can easily modify the rides with the aid of either a road
atlas or, where off-road routes are involved, an Ordnance Survey map
for the area.

Rides for everybody

Cycling is ideal for almost any age and ability. In central Cheshire, on
any Sunday morning, you're bound to see large groups of cyclists from
local clubs going for a fifty-mile spin before lunch. In the Peak District
foothills, you'll see mountain men out of their saddles, straining up hills
that the family car can only tackle in bottom gear. But you'll also find
small groups and lone cyclists exploring country lanes, visiting friends,
seeking out places of interest and generally having a good time. Those
are the people that will get the most from this book (though there are
some 'challenge rides' for those who get too cocky!)

Sketch maps provided, but . . .

There's no substitute for Ordnance Survey (OS) maps and that's why we
have specified the appropriate OS Landranger (1:50,000 scale) at the start
of each route. The routes are accompanied by rough sketch maps, but
these are only intended as a very rough planning aid. If you have OS
Pathfinder or Outdoor Leisure maps (both 1:25,000 scale), by all means
use them, but you will find that cycling covers much greater distances

than walking, so you'll constantly be folding and re-folding these maps and running off the edges of them. When using OS maps, some people find it useful to use a clip-on map holder on their handlebars; alternatively, use the type that ramblers sling around their necks, though you'll need to stop from time-to-time to check directions. A simple compass is useful if you're planning your own rides, especially if they involve off-road work. Again, the type favoured by ramblers is ideal.

What Sort of Bike?

Hills and Gears

You'll not get very far, and certainly not enjoy your cycling, unless your bike has an adequate range of gears. As a minimum, the three-speed or four-speed Sturmey-Archer (or Far Eastern equivalent) is perfectly OK for flatter and modestly-hilly rides. For anything more ambitious, five- to ten-speed (or so) Derailleur gears offer more flexibility. Oddly enough, a ten-speed version is not necessarily twice as good as a five, because there is quite a lot of overlap between the ratios: most of the time you end up using a couple at either end of the gear ranges, but the very lowest ratios make steep Cheshire hills a doddle (except for such challenges as the road up to "The Edge" from Alderley, and many around Bollington, but you'll soon find out!)

Mountain bikes

A world of their own! Many mountain bikers are to be seen in the latest Lycra gear, covered in mud from head to toe – and having fun! Mountain bikes can, however, be useful for general touring and for tackling any of the rides in this book. The fatter, squashier, tyres soak up the bumps and pot-holes and the wide range of gear ratios (often 20 or more) means that you'll hardly ever have to push your bike up a hill. They are, however, more expensive than the average tourer-style of bike.

Hire a Bike or Use your Own?

Convenience and choice

Naturally, you'll want to tackle the cycle rides that are most convenient for you. But when you have exhausted these, there are two options: take your bike with you or hire when you get there. Hiring makes a lot of sense because it avoids lots of hassle and might enable you to select the type of bike most appropriate to the ride (e.g. a mountain bike for The Peak District). But this all needs careful planning, so only you can decide what is best for you.

Taking your own bike

... by car

With a car, you can sometimes simply put down the rear seats and put it in the back. Or, invest in a cycle carrier that will transport a couple of bikes either on top of the car or suspended from the rear. The latter needs to be fitted correctly to avoid damage to either the car or bike; take professional advice from a reputable supplier.

... by public transport

Many of the routes in this book start from a town with a railway station. This is because stations are usually well-signposted and centrally-located. Also, a train is

Bike Hire in Cheshire

At the time of writing, there is no centralised information service on bike hire in the county. For the most current information, contact your local T.I.C. or phone the Heritage and Recreation section of Cheshire County Council on 01244-602843; the Tourism Attractions section on 01244-603127 may also be able to help.

Wherever you hire a bike, remember that you will need proof of identity (e.g. driving licence) and a deposit for each cycle. Check that bikes are available and, especially for groups, book bikes in advance. Some centres (e.g. Tatton) hire tandems and 'duets' (wheelchair tandems for the disabled)

The Groundwork Trust operate bike hire schemes at Tatton Park (near Knutsford), Delamere Forest (Forestry Commission Discovery Centre, Linmere, on the A556 between Chester and Northwich) and Bollington (Adelphi Mill, Grimshaw Lane, Bollington, near Macclesfield). Cycle hire centres are open every weekend, Easter to October, Bank Holidays, and every day in July and August; Bollington and Delamere open from 10 am, Tatton from 10.30 to 11 am, and all hires close at 6 pm; party bookings are welcome and hires can be arranged outside normal times. Contact the Groundwork Trust on 01625-572681.

Other cycle hirers include:

South Cheshire Cycle Hire (01829-271242) for Farndon and surrounding areas.

Davies Bros (cycles) Ltd, 6 Cuppin Street, Chester CH1 2BN. Tel: 01244-319204; Chester area, summer only.

a convenient way of travelling around Cheshire (and perhaps hiring a bike at your destination) but can be even better if you are taking your bike with you. The regulations concerning bicycles on trains are currently: Inter City trains carry a maximum of three bikes and reservations should be made in advance as certain services carry no bikes at all; other trains (including Sprinters) carry bikes under protest and it is always advisable to reserve space; for peace of mind, phone

British Rail in advance, smile nicely at the station staff, and you should be OK.

Buses in Cheshire do not, as a general rule, carry bikes.

General Points

Maintenance

Bikes are often neglected and can easily become unreliable or unsafe. Some obvious point to check include:

Brakes – check that the brake pads are in good order and that they are adjusted to be within a millimetre or so of the wheel rim. To check the brakes, push the bike along and apply the front brake; the wheel should 'lock' and the bike will be immobilised. Do the same with the rear brake applied while leaning on the saddle; the rear wheel should remain stationary and skid as you try to push.

Tyres and wheels – see that there is a reasonable tread on the tyres or you will be constantly suffering from punctures (thorns on the road easily penetrate a thin tyre, especially when wet). Think about investing in 'Kevlar'-lined tyres or buy the linings separately – you'll then enjoy puncture-free cycling. Check the wheels for broken spokes and lack of buckling.

Bearings – The bottom bracket bearing (the one that the pedal crank rotates in) often becomes loose or worn; in severe cases, the crank may jam, so check the bearing by moving the pedals at right angles to the frame – there should be scarcely any play. Similarly, check the head bracket (on the handlebar stem) and adjust as necessary.

Bells and horns – though not a legal requirement, if fitted they should work. Horns are more effective, if only to alert careless pedestrians – and they can even make your complaints audible to those car drivers who don't seem able to see cyclists.

Lights – a cyclist riding without lights at night is extremely vulnerable. And if you start a ride on a winter's afternoon, how can you be sure of getting back in daylight? Be sure to fit efficient lights (or carry them with you if you don't want to have them stolen) and check them regularly.

If you're not happy about any of this, *please* visit your local bike shop.

Comfort & safety

Cheshire weather is not always perfect for cycling, despite the idyllic cover of this book. Therefore, it is wise to carry some form of waterproofs and, if style's your thing, invest in the highly attractive and practical clothing now available for cyclists. Some of the colours might seem lurid, but their visibility is a safety bonus. Supplement this for night-time cycling with reflective bands.

Protective headgear is not yet required by law, but the new lightweight helmets have become widely accepted and are worth considering, especially for younger cyclists with little experience of busy roads and careless drivers.

Security

'Lock it or lose it' is the best advice. Invest in a lock and chain, and always park your bike where it can be seen, chained to a lamp-post or similar immovable object. Remove items such as a pump or lamp and leave nothing of value in panniers. Consider having your bike security-marked by the police and keep a note of its serial number (usually stamped on the frame) separate from the bike itself.

Spares and repairs

So far, nobody has come up with the bicycle equivalent of an AA man (though older readers may remember Monty Python's Bicycle Repair Man). So, always be sure to take a spare inner tube and a set of tools so that you can keep mobile. Don't even think about repairing a puncture until you get home. A few standard spanners, oddments such as spare light bulbs and some common sense will come in handy for minor repairs and adjustments. In desperation, since our rides all start at reasonably-sized towns, you may find a handy cycle shop or, more likely, an obliging garage to get you out of trouble.

When your bike is in need of repair, remember that most cycle shops are quite small and many are one-man bands, so service 'on demand' is unlikely. But being a regular might just pay off!

Children

Don't expect to give a bike to a child and expect that all will be well; in fact, don't expect to see them again in the same state that they left you. Britain's roads were not designed for cyclists, and children do not have the experience to predict what a motorist might do: open the door in their path, drive in front of them, stop suddenly, or just not see them. Therefore, all young cyclists must be accompanied by an experienced adult cyclist until they can demonstrate mastery. Also, enrol your child on a Cycling Proficiency course at their school and make it clear that he or she won't be allowed out without you until they pass. Sometimes, local voluntary organisations such as Cubs or Brownies run the courses and the County Road Safety Officer should be able to tell you who's running what – but make a fuss if you can't find one. Even better, get involved in running one yourself – it's hard work (I know, I used to run one) and very worthwhile; naturally, you and your helpers have to be approved by the County Council, but the red tape is fairly minimal.

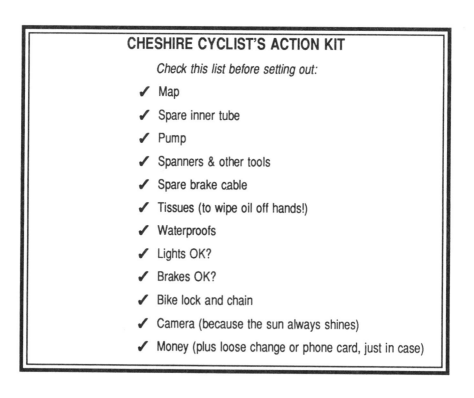

CHESHIRE CYCLIST'S ACTION KIT

Check this list before setting out:

✓ Map

✓ Spare inner tube

✓ Pump

✓ Spanners & other tools

✓ Spare brake cable

✓ Tissues (to wipe oil off hands!)

✓ Waterproofs

✓ Lights OK?

✓ Brakes OK?

✓ Bike lock and chain

✓ Camera (because the sun always shines)

✓ Money (plus loose change or phone card, just in case)

Take care, and enjoy your cycling!

1. Adlington to Whiteley Green

Distance: 13 miles/21km

Route: Adlington Station – Booth Green – Skellorn Green – Wards End – Middlewood Way – Whiteley Green – Adlington Station.

Surface: Tarmac and gravel.

Start: Adlington Station (SJ912803)

Map: O.S. Landranger 109 (Manchester and surrounding area) and O.S. 118 (the Potteries).

The Route

This short ride is ideal for a family ride. The hills are quite modest and you should find no difficulty in completing the 13 miles and, perhaps, another in the same day. There are pleasant views of the Cheshire plain with distant hills beyond. About 3 miles of the route passes along the Middlewood Way. This was once a railway line and is now a scenic nature trail used by walkers, cyclists and horse riders.

There are two pubs: the Legh Arms, at the start point, and The Windmill, just off the Middlewood Way. Adlington Hall is passed at the very end of the route. The hall itself is well worth a visit and there are occasional classical concerts and craft fairs. (note: hall normally open only on Bank Holidays and Sundays).

Adlington Station is the start of the route and cyclists who use their cars to get to the start point should park in the layby near to the Legh Arms.

The Journey

Section a-b

With the Legh Arms on your left, leave Adlington Station and turn right. Cycle for about a mile, past Adlington Primary School, and then turn left onto Roundy Lane. At the top of this lane, at the second 'Give Way' sign, turn left onto Cawley Lane. Soon Cawley Lane becomes Skellorn Green

Lane. Likewise, Skellorn Green Lane changes to Wood Lane West after a right-hand bend with Hope Lane on your left.

Turn left onto Moggy Lane and follow the road up to Waterloo Road. Turn right here and cycle up to the T-junction. Now turn right into Coppice Road and continue past the 'late shop' on your left and over a bridge. After the bridge follow the road up to a car park on your right. Turn into the car park and pass through the opening in front of you – you are now on the Middlewood Way and you should turn left.

Section b-c

The Middlewood Way is a disused railway track, renovated by Macclesfield Borough Council. The two new track-ways are used by both

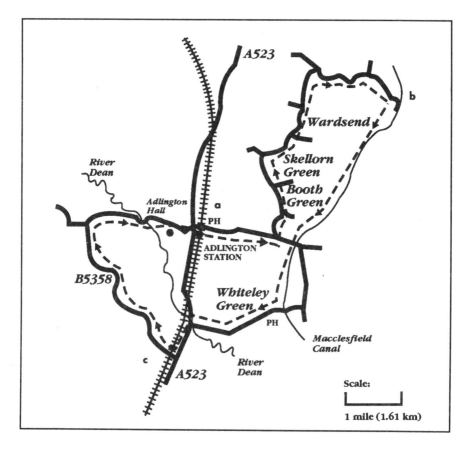

cyclists and walkers, so take care. By going through the opening (described in a-b) you will be cycling on the path to the right of the Middlewood Way. On this side there are picnic tables and benches where you can sit and admire the view.

Leave the Middlewood Way after you have gone under the fifth bridge (Holehouse Lane). Carry your bike up the steps on your right and go through the opening onto the road.

Section c-a

At the top of Middlewood Way head left and go past the Windmill Pub on your left. Keep to this road until a T-junction after a bridge. Turn left here onto the A523 and cycle up to Prestbury. Take the first turn to the right, Bonis Hall Lane, and go under the railway bridge. Follow this road for about two miles until you reach Mill Lane on your right.

Turn here and you will soon come to a crossroads after passing Adlington Hall on your right. Go straight across the A523, past the Legh Arms Pub, and back to the Station on your right.

Adlington Hall

2. Alderley Edge and Gawsworth

Distance: 25 miles/40km.

Route: Alderley Edge – Row of Trees – Lindow End – Chelford – Siddington Heath – Marton – Gawsworth – Lower Pexhill – Henbury Hall – Birtles Hall – Over Alderley – Mottram St Andrew – The Hough – Alderley Edge.

Surface: Tarmac, Grass and Gravel.

Start: Alderley Edge Railway Station (SJ843786).

Map: O.S. 118 (the Potteries).

The Route

This circular, long-distance ride uses a network of quiet lanes on either side of the A34 on the perimeter of the Cheshire plain, bordered by Alderley Edge to the north, Macclesfield to the east and Congleton to the south. The ride in its entirety takes between 3 – 5 hours and is best suited to longer and stronger legs, though individual sections can be attempted and enjoyed by families with young cyclists.

Two of Cheshire's best-known stately homes, Capesthorne and Gawsworth Hall (both privately owned but partially open to the public and worth visiting) fall within this ride which also takes you through National Trust Land on Alderley Edge.

The hillier ground to the North East of the ride should not prove unduly difficult and the route is well-supplied with pubs, tea shops and pleasant picnic spots. Hedgerows and hilly views improve with walking!

Some of the lanes are narrow and twisting and, although they may not appear so, frequented by the occasional car and tractor, so it is unwise to be complacent. The ride starts and finishes at Alderley Edge Railway Station. For those who hate paying for the privilege of parking here, it is sometimes possible to find unrestricted parking in the village side streets, or the car parks of the Moss Rose and Royal Oak pubs in Heyes Lane (leaving the station on the south-bound, Crewe side) which you will no doubt patronise during the course of your ride. Note that Tom Royle's cycle shop, which used to be in Brook Lane, has now relocated to the Wilmslow end of Knutsford Road, half a mile or so away.

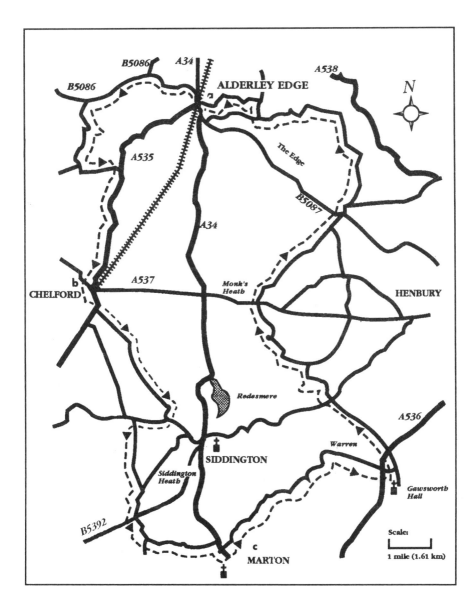

The Journey

Section a-b

Leave the station car park, turn right onto Heyes Lane, then right again onto the A34. (*The road is very busy and it may be safer to walk to the pedestrian crossing five metres away, cross the road and begin cycling from there.*) Whichever you choose, now head towards Wilmslow.

Cross the railway bridge and take the second left, into Brook Lane (B5085). Continue for just over a mile, passing Alderley Edge Golf Club on your right and going over a mini-roundabout. Continue for a further mile, passing Prospect House hotel on your right, Foden Lane on your left and then turn left into Warford Lane.

Follow Warford Lane as it dips to cross a brook and rises to run alongside Wilmslow Golf Club on the left, then round a sharp left-hand bend into Great Warford. Note the tiny brick Baptist Chapel, converted from a barn and cottage in 1712 and the attractive Warford Crescent. At the T-junction with the A535, turn right and continue for 1½ miles, passing under a railway line (watch out for traffic lights) to the roundabout at Chelford.

Section b-c

Leave the roundabout by the A535 (signposted to Holmes Chapel). The road is flanked on the right by Astle Park and on the left by the grounds of Capesthorne Hall. In the first edition of this book, we continued to the second turn left along Lapwing Lane but this is no longer passable due to quarry expansion. *Here are the new instructions:* Starting from the roundabout, take the first left turn along Congleton Lane. Continue for 2 miles then make a sharp right hairpin into Whisterfield Lane. After half a mile, take a left hairpin into Chapel Lane. *The original route now continues:* Continue down Chapel Lane and over a crossroads with the B5392. After 100 metres, turn right down a wide grassy track signed as "Boundary Lane". At a farmhouse on the right, the grass gives way to a gravel surface.

Where this rejoins the road, having caught a fleeting glimpse of the British Telecom tower on Croker Hill, above Wincle (to the east), turn right, cross Red Lion Brook and continue for half a mile before turning left into Davenport Lane.

Continue, enjoying tantalizing snatches of The Cloud in the distance (see route 16) and test your brakes before the road descends quickly to a T-junction with the A34 just north of Marton.

Turn right. Relief is at hand. Beyond the garage on the right is the Davenport Arms and immediately ahead on the left are Marton Church and Marton Farm Shop Tea Rooms. Thus, spiritual and physical refreshment are provided on the southernmost point of the journey.

Section c-a

From now on the route is homeward-bound. Double back on yourself, leaving Marton Church behind you and take the first right, Oak Lane, which winds round Marton and joins the road to Warren at a T-junction by Marton Primary School.

Turn right into Marton Lane and pass a soft-fruit farm and Pikelow Farm where trout fishing is available, should you have your rods with you. Continue for 3 miles. Just before the crossroads with the A536 the square tower of Gawsworth Church is visible above the trees. Cross the A536 and go into Maggotty Lane, past Maggotty Johnson's grave.

At the next crossroads you can either:

– turn right to visit Gawsworth Hall and Church half a mile away. In the *Buildings of England* series Sir Niklaus Pevsner, in an uncharacteristic rush of enthusiasm for the county, said of Gawsworth:

> *"There is nothing in Cheshire to compare with the loveliness of the church above the pool and the three great houses and one small house grouped around two further pools."*

which will surely tempt you to linger.

– or, stick to the route, and turn left again into Church Lane. Cross the A536 into Dark Lane. Note the Old Police Cottage on the left-hand corner. After crossing a brook the road rises to a staggered crossroads (approx. one mile) with the Siddington - Broken Cross road. Turn right and almost immediately left into Bearhurst Lane.

There's just time to catch a glimpse of the 18th-century stable block to the former Henbury Hall before the road descends beyond Bearhurst Farm into a wooded gully – Huntly Wood – thick with bluebells in the Spring.

Shakespearian performance at Gawsworth Hall

At the T-junction opposite the entrance to Henbury Hall, turn left and at the crest of the hill, opposite a farm, right into an unmarked lane which descends steeply to join the A537, after a mile, at another T-junction.

Continue over and up Birtles lane passing Birtles Hall and Church. The gradient is deceptive – it looks reasonably level but the surface has an uncanny ability to slow bike tyres down. Never mind, it's a very pretty walk!

Continue uphill, over a small crossroads and past Over Alderley Methodist Church on your left, to the T-junction with the B5087 (2 miles). The Black Greyhound Smithy will be on your right. Turn right and take the second left in about 25 yards. This is narrow, dark and twisting, and ends at best in a T-junction, at worst in tears. Turn right and then take the first left into Oak Lane.

Shortly after a sign on the left warning against horse-riding on the verges, the road narrows to squeeze around the side of a house on the right. Oncoming traffic is not visible from here. If you have horns, bells or a good singing voice, now is the time to use them!

In 1$^1/_2$ miles, you reach a T-junction, where you turn left into Alderley Road, passing Mottram St Andrew Methodist Chapel on the left and continuing past the National Trust's entrance to the Old Mines on the Edge, also on the left.

Approximately a third of a mile after the Alderley Edge boundary sign and the tiny brick and half-timbered barn on the left, turn right into Hough Lane. Take the first left into Moss Road and left again into Heyes Lane (half a mile). The entrance to the Moss Rose car park is immediately on your left. If you go fast here, you'll miss it!

The ends is in sight: continue past the Public Library and Royal Oak Pub on your left and in 200 yards you're back at the railway station where you started.

3. Alderley Edge, Henbury and The Edge

Distance: 10 miles/16km.

Route: The Edge – Nether Alderley – Henbury – Over Alderley – The Edge.

Surface: Tarmac, Gravel and Cobbles (!)

Start: The Edge Car Park (SJ859773).

Map: O.S. 118 (the Potteries).

The Route

This short ride using quiet lanes and bridleways south west of Alderley Edge is picturesque and undemanding. The highest point of the ride is at the start on the Edge.

The Blacksmiths Arms at Henbury is the only refreshment point on the route and would make a good alternative start point.

Mountain bike tyres might make less of a meal of the cobbled and gravel sections of bridleway, but these are not uncycleable with conventional touring wheels. If you get anxious about rim trueness and spoke tension – walk!

There are toilet facilities at the start point and the ride can easily be completed within 1 – 1$^1/_2$ hours.

The Journey

Section a-b

Leave the car park and turn right onto the B5087. In 20 yards, turn left opposite the Wizard Restaurant, down Artists Lane. (The restaurant does not have a bar. It's a full-blown meal or nothing!).

Pass Wizard Tree Farms on the left (Christmas trees in season) and descend through an arcade of beech trees. Turn left at the T-junction onto the A34 and left again at the phone box up Bradford Lane (an

The Wizard

RUPP – 'road used as a public path') whose broken surface rapidly gives way to neat, hard cobbles.

Where the lane divides, take the right fork (signed 'Private Road and Bridle Path') leading to Hocker Lane. To prevent the excitement of being to able to cycle so fast on the by-now gravel surface from going to your head, four sleeping policemen lie in wait.

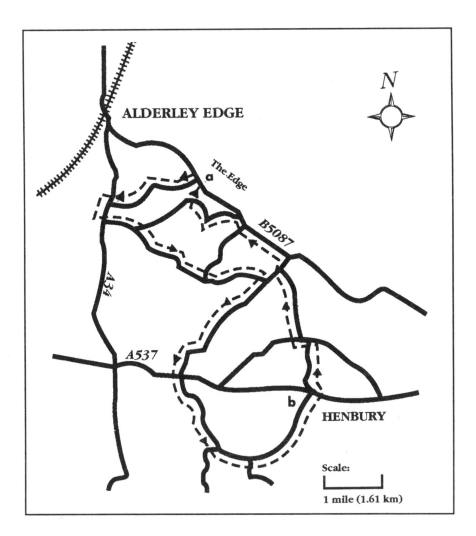

At the end, go straight across onto Hocker Lane (not named at this end), ignoring Slade Lane to the left. Tarmac once more! At the crossroads, turn right down Birtles Lane, catching views, to the right, of Jodrell Bank, Birtles Church and Birtles Hall.

Cross the A537 and climb the lane opposite, signposted 'Pexhill 2 miles'. Continue and, at the top, opposite a brick-built farm, turn left. Continue to the crossroads on the A537. The Blacksmiths Arms is on the left-hand corner.

Section b-a

Cross the A537 (with care) and climb Pepper Street. Turn left at the top into Andertons Lane. At the T-Junction turn left, then first right into aptly-named Wrigley Lane.

Continue over a small crossroads and, at a T-junction, turn right past Over Alderley Methodist Church.

Continue to the end and turn left onto the B5087, at the smithy. After a crossroads with Slade Lane and School Lane, turn left obliquely along Finlow Hill Lane. (This isn't essential, but cuts off a half-mile stretch of road that can be busy). The lane curves round to rejoin the B5087: keep Finlow Hill wood on your right and then turn right into Bradford Lane. Turn left when you rejoin the B5087 and continue for 200 yards to the start point on the right.

4. Alsager: Hassall Green & Scholar Green

Distance: 19 miles/30km

Route: Alsager – Lawton Heath End – Hassall Green – Spen Green – Brownlow Heath – Ackers Crossing – Scholar Green – Church Lawton – Alsager

Surface: Tarmac

Start: Alsager Railway Station (SJ802552)

Map: O.S. 118 (the Potteries).

The Route

This very gentle ride is, for the most part, firmly set on the Cheshire Plain but in its latter half flirts with the hills that skirt it, and should only take an hour or two to complete. Aside from the simple delights of the Cheshire countryside, much of this ride's attraction lies in the hostelries that line it – those mentioned in the text are those worthy of special note.

In terms of distance and gradients, this ride is very suitable for a family, but care should be taken at the numerous points where an A-road has to be crossed, as this is considerably more dangerous than riding along them.

The Journey

Cycling north from the railway station towards the town centre, continue straight across the junction in the middle of the town such that you're heading out of Alsager along the B5078. After passing the Wilbraham Arms and cycling through a gap in the old Salt Line, turn left down a narrow lane before the road you are on joins another.

This brings you to Hassall Green, home to the Romping Donkey where you should bear right and continue on past the now disused village school. This soon brings you to a crossroads overlooked by the New Inn – carry straight on, with care, as this is a deceptively fast road. This in turn brings you to another A-road, where you should again continue straight on. The lane you now find yourself in will take you past a church, St John's, a recording studio and the highly recommended Blue Bell Inn in Spen Green.

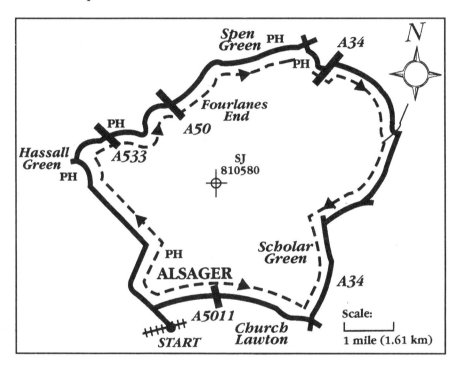

Shortly after passing some large commercial greenhouses, and immediately after cycling over the brow of a small hill, turn right to head down past the Brownlow Inn, such that the prominent feature on the horizon switches from being the Cloud to the Mow Cop folly. This brings you to the A34, which you should turn left onto and then swiftly right off from, as soon as you've passed the garage.

Follow this lane up the hill, past Great Moreton Hall (which is now a hotel) and over the canal at Ackers Crossing, such that you're in the shadow of Mow Cop. As you join another road, turn right over the canal and then continue on down the hill into Scholar Green. Turning left onto the A34, make your way past the Rising Sun, the Traveller's Rest and the Bleeding Wolf until you find yourself dropping down to a set of traffic lights at which you should turn right.

Follow this road over the canal and then across the A5011, back into Alsager; from there make your way back to the railway station where you began.

5. Ashley (near Knutsford) to Tatton Park, Rostherne and Arley

Distance: 15 miles/23 km.

Route: Ashley or Tatton Park – Rostherne – Bucklow Hill – Hoo Green – Arley Green – Moss End – Bate Heath – Tabley Hill – Tatton Park.

Surface: Tarmac, grass and cobbled, also can be muddy.

Start: Ashley station (SJ773843) or Tatton Park.

Map: O.S. Landranger 109 (Manchester and surrounding area) and O.S. 118 (the Potteries).

The Route

This ride uses quiet country lanes and bridleways and only occasionally strays onto main roads. It's a middle-distance ride – not too demanding as there are no gruelling uphill climbs. There are two pubs on the route, and Arley Hall and Tatton Park also provide refreshments.

The ride begins at Ashley Station, about 2 miles away from Tatton Park, which is an alternative start point,.

On leaving Ashley Station, turn right and follow the road round a few sharp corners, down past a stream and up into a wooded area. Once through here, you will see a long straight road. After about $3/4$ of a mile, turn into the entrance of Tatton Park which is the start point of the main part of the ride.

You can hire bikes at Tatton Park for around £5 (less for half a day – see introduction for details); Cars are charged £2.00 admission to the park but pedestrians and cyclists get in for free.

The Journey

Section a-b

Leave the main entrance to Tatton Park, cross over the road and head down towards Rostherne. You soon reach this small and attractive village with several quaint buildings on your right.

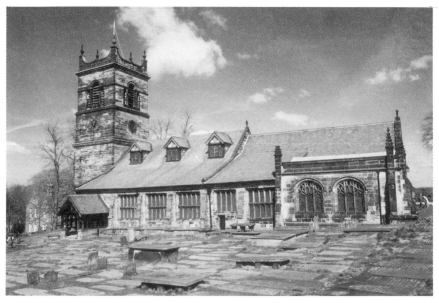

Rostherne church

Take the next road on your left. Continue past a lake on the left, and uphill through a shady, protective overhang of trees. As you reach the end of this road, turn right and head towards the traffic lights with the Swan Inn on your right and a BP Garage on your left.

Cycle over the busy A556 towards Bucklow Hill Garage on the right, and immediately turn left down Chapel Lane. (If you are with younger cyclists you might be best advised to walk this part of the route!)

Follow this road past Bucklow Hill Reform Church on the right, then take the first left turn into Hulse Heath Road. Follow this road, passing

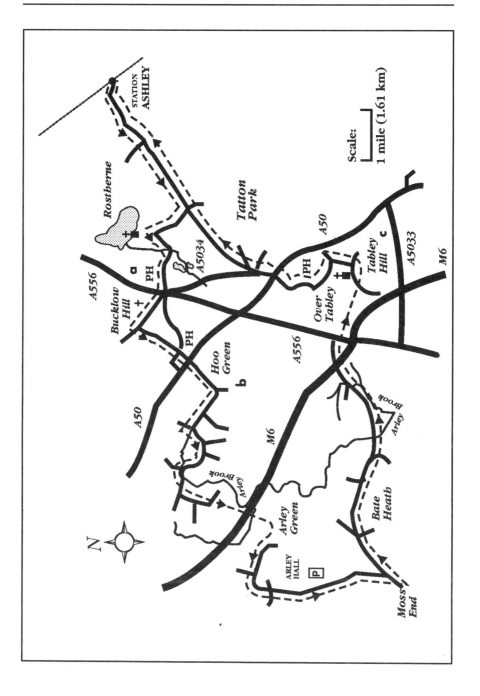

Bowden View Lane on your right, and then go right at the T-junction. Follow this short road to the A50 at Hoo Green with the Kilton Pub on your left and a Shell garage on the other side of the A50 to the left. Cycle across this road and onto Hoo Green Lane.

Section b-c

Follow this road all the way round, past Goodiers Green Farm and Rowleybank Farm until you reach the bottom of Whitley Lane (Hoo Green Lane changes to Whitley Lane en route). Turn right here and continue until you reach Golborne Lane on your left; turn down here.

Continue until you reach Northwood Lane; turn left here and follow the road past Hope House and Hobs Hill Lane, both on your right. The road soon takes a sharp left by Northwood Cottage, but you must leave the road here and proceed onto the bridleway straight ahead.

Follow the bridleway straight down, through a narrow opening and over a motorway bridge. Continue on the other side, past a gate to another bridleway on the left. The path narrows here, continuing through trees until you reach a small gate on the left with a "Private" sign. Opposite this gate is a small iron gate leading into a field.

Follow the track to the left of the trees and head towards the far right-hand corner of the field. At the end of this track, go through another small gate and onto a road which leads up to Arley Hall. Turn right here and follow it all the way round to a crossroads.

At this point either:

– Turn left to visit Arley Hall and Gardens; a superb historic site owned by the Warburton family since medieval times.

– Or, cross over the road and, after a mile or so, turn right at the bottom of the road. Continue along this road to Georges Lane, which is directly opposite.

Turn left onto Budworth Road, past Moss End Cottage on your left, and follow the road into Bate Heath. At the next left turning – Conn Lane – there is an 18th century building 'The Pinfold, Aston-By-Budworth'. This isn't much to look at, but is of some interest: a pinfold was where stray cattle were kept in a pen, to be released (for a payment) to their rightful owners.

Continue down the same road you were on and then over Arley Brook and past Heyrose Golf Club on the left. Take the next left onto Old Hall Lane and follow this road over another motorway bridge and down to the A556 once again. Proceed with caution over the A556, heading slightly to the left to get onto the next bridleway.

Watch out for debris and continue past a poultry farm on the left, up to a small gate at the far end of the field, where the track ends. Once through the gate, turn left onto Tetley Road and head up towards Tabley Hill cemetery on your left. Stop here and admire the beauty of this country church.

Section c-a

Take the next left onto Green Lane and continue past the masses of rose-beds on the left-hand side. Take another left onto Moss Lane, with tranquil ponds either side. Follow this road, soon taking a sharp right bend, with Moss Side Cottage on you left. Avoid the left turning here and continue cycling past a row of luxury houses on your left.

Soon you arrive at the A50 again. Cross over the road here and head down the road opposite. Follow this road as far as the "Q8" Garage. Turn right before the garage and head back to Tatton Park, looking out for the Deer Park on the right.

In days gone by, such parks were actively used for deer hunting and the penalties were severe if a peasant helped himself. Nowadays, these beautiful animals wander peacefully at Tatton.

6. Beeston, Barnhill & Peckforton

Distance: 11 miles/17.5km.

Route: Beeston Castle car park – Barnhill – Gallantry Bank – Peckforton
– Beeston – Beeston Castle car park.

Surface: Country roads, tracks, small part main road.

Start: Beeston Castle car park (SJ538592).

Map: O.S. 117 (Chester).

The Route

This is a relatively short route of only 11 miles. The area is very
attractive, but quite remote and, as there are no train stations nearby,
you'll need your own transport.

The two main attractions in the area are Peckforton Castle and Beeston
Castle which both overlook the Cheshire Plain and can be seen for many
miles around. Beeston Castle is now a small ruin, as a result of over 700
years of weathering and decay. However, Peckforton Castle which was
built just 150 years ago, is still in perfect condition. This would be well
worth a visit and guided tours are available. Ring the Castle for opening
times on (01829) 260930.

The Journey

Section a-b

Leave Beeston Castle car park (opposite the main entrance) and turn
right. Follow the road round with Beeston Castle on your left. Ignore
turnings to the right and, at the T-junction, turn right. The road soon
bears sharply to the left. Follow the track (signed for a 'dead end') which
carries straight on.

After a house on the left, the track deteriorates; continue over a railway
bridge and here the terrain becomes quite overgrown and narrow. Cross

over a stream via a large stone and then bear right once you reach a field. Go through a small gate in the corner of the field, remembering to close it behind you.

Turn left onto another track and, where the road forks, go left and continue under a railway bridge. At the bottom of this track, turn left onto a quiet country road. Follow this road past Oakfield Farm on the left and up to a crossroads. Turn right and, after half a mile, take the first left down a long narrow lane. At the bottom of this lane, follow the road round to the right just before Beehive Farm. At the end of this road, turn right at the T-junction and then immediately turn left.

At the next T-junction, turn left. At the end of this road there is another T-junction. Turn left here and then take the first right turn.

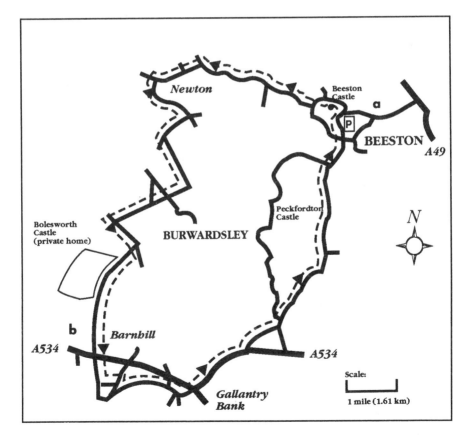

Section b-a

Follow this road for a mile and a half and, after a short downhill descent, you reach the A534. Go straight on at the crossroads into Hill lane, take the next left onto Broom Hill Lane and you are now in the small village of Barnhill. At the bottom of Broom Hill lane turn right at the T-junction and then take the next left down the unusually-named Reading Room Lane. Follow this road for three-quarters of a mile and, at the bottom of the road, turn right opposite the tennis courts. When you reach Bickerton Holy Trinity Church, turn left down Brunty Bank, and follow this up to the main road (A534).

Turn right here and continue for another three quarters of a mile until the first turning on the left, following signs for Beeston Castle. Carry on for almost three miles, passing through the village of Peckforton and past Peckforton Castle. At the end of this road, turn left and then almost immediately turn right and follow the road back up to Beeston Castle car park on the right.

Beeston Castle

7. Bollington, Pott Shrigley & Kerridge

Distance: Whole ride: 11 miles/17.5km; First Leg: 6 miles/9.5km; Second Leg: 6 miles/9.5km.

Route: Middlewood Way – Pott Shrigley – Rainow – Bollington – Kerridge – Higher Hurdsfield – Hurdsfield Industrial Estate – Middlewood Way.

Surface: Track and Tarmac.

Start: Middlewood Way car park, near Peaks and Plains Discovery Centre, Grimshaw Lane, Bollington (SJ930775).

Map: O.S. Landranger 109 (Manchester and surrounding area) and O.S. 118 (the Potteries).

The Route

This very strenuous route goes through some of Cheshire's most attractive rolling countryside. It is a hard route to do in one go, but because it loops in and out of Bollington, it is quite feasible to split into two, and still see some wonderful scenery. See map for details. The hills make the ride quite hard, but the second of the two parts eliminate the worst of these.

Like the Poynton ride, the route makes excellent use of The Middlewood Way; there is also some quite busy road riding, although this is minimised and country lanes have been used wherever possible.

You may well meet horseriders on The Middlewood Way, so don't upset the horses. One should also be wary of the 'extras' emanating from horses!

Please note the map details above.

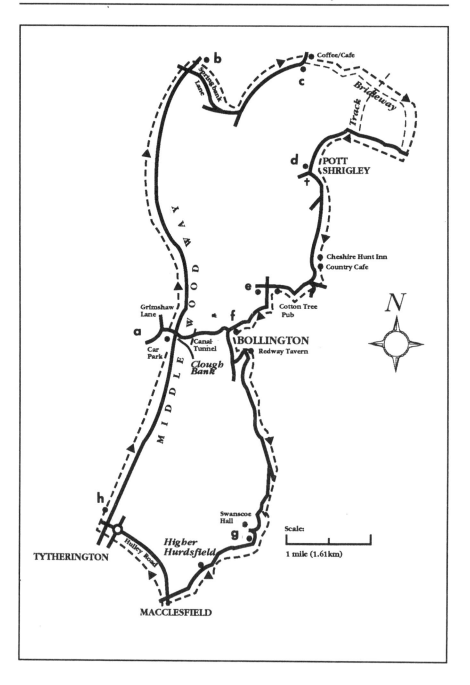

The Journey

Section a-b

Our route begins at the car park for the Middlewood Way at Clough Bank, Bollington. This is located just before the Groundwork Trust Information Centre, where you can also hire cycles.

If you are doing either the whole ride or the first leg, join the Middlewood Way *on the other side of Grimshaw Lane*, and follow it northwards for about 2¹/₂ miles. This might seem a long distance, but the surroundings more than justify this as you roughly follow the canal tow path. Look out for the Street Lane bridge sign, and emerge onto *Springbank Lane* (surely a mistake!). *If you are doing the second leg only*, please turn to the First/Second Leg section.

Section b-c

Turn right at the top of the steps onto the road and go over the bridge, immediately passing Springbank Farm on your left.

Follow the road to its end and turn left, taking care as this is on a bend, although you should be able to see OK. Keep going along here as it twists and turns for just over half a mile, up to another 'corner' junction. Here, turn left again, following the sign to Pott Shrigley.

Pass a farm on your left, and follow this picturesque lane for about ²/₃ mile, where it goes into a fairly sharp left bend. On the right of this bend, a Bridleway sign marks our route. However, you may choose to break your route here, and follow the road just a few more yards to a quiet roadside cafe (The Coffee Tavern), which serves a range of snacks and drinks.

Section c-d

Having re-commenced your route, go back to the Bridlepath and go up it – 'up' being the operative word! It is quite a steep track initially, and many may need to dismount and walk. It continues to rise right up to a once-magnificent set of farm buildings at Birchencliff; there once was the intention to develop this as up-market cottages.

Keep to your route as it goes downhill for a short distance to a gate. Through the gate, go uphill again, although the first part of this is the only hard part.

The old community at Birchencliff

As the track/bridleway goes on, it bends to what, at the time of writing, is a very old and rickety gate. Once through this gate, you will see a signpost marking a footpath and bridleway. To shorten the route slightly and leave another climb out, dismount and follow the track/footpath to the right. This goes over a cattlegrid and out onto a quiet tarmac road, which, in turn, emerges out onto the main route again. Turn right here and follow the road downhill to Pott Shrigley church and school. It could also be wise, during lambing seasons to follow the footpath route (having dismounted), as this would minimise disturbance to the sheep.

However, to carry on, follow the bridleway up the hill and then down a fairly steep hill to a gate (follow the bridleway signs and waymarks), and out onto the road. Follow this steeply downhill (your previous work being rewarded) to Pott Shrigley church and school. Note that this road is both narrow and well-used by cars!

Section d-e

At the church, turn left and head back south towards Bollington. Take the first road on the left, which is more of a 'straight-on' than a turn left!

Follow this road along, gently climbing for a while, until you drop more sharply, over a bridge and into the outskirts of Rainow. On your left, pass the Cheshire Hunt Inn and the Country Cafe (or stop!). Follow the hill and take a right turn at the triangular junction, but prepare to stop immediately, as you come to a Give Way sign. *This takes you by surprise,* being just over the brow of the hill.

Head right again, dropping down towards Bollington, through Sowcar (blink, and you'll miss it).

Section e-f

Pass the Cotton Tree pub, and then take a *sharp* left into Church Street at the Shrigley Road junction. Wind around the back parts of Bollington, passing a church and industrial works, and ride or – more likely – walk up another hill. Turn right at the very top of this and follow the road round a left bend. The road becomes Chancery Lane and is very narrow; continue to its end.

First/Second Legs

It is at this point that the first and second legs finish and start respectively. If you are only doing the first leg, you get good reward for your labours by simply turning right at this junction and following the road downhill, under the canal, past the Groundwork Trust, and left into Clough Bank and the car park. Do take care on the slope, for it is steep, and the road can be quite busy.

If however, you are joining the ride at this point, covering the second leg, you need to leave the car park and go out of Clough Bank, turning right onto Grimshaw Lane, under the canal, and up the steep hill. The road will eventually lead you to the junction of Chancery Lane and Jackson Lane, and by going right into the latter, you have joined the ride.

Section f-g

From Chancery Lane, you effectively carry on, the road becoming Jackson Lane, and heading out towards Kerridge. After about a quarter of a mile you pass a small chapel, and then another quarter mile on, take a very sharp left at The Bulls Head pub into Redway; go past the Redway Tavern, round another very sharp bend, and up quite a steep hill. The road soon flattens out, and we continue along here for about three-quarters mile. This is a fairly quiet lane, and when cars do come, they are generally not racing along.

A road goes off to the left, but we stay on Kerridge Road, and follow it down the hill, winding towards its conclusion. Again, take care as it is very easy to pick up dangerous amounts of speed. At the bottom of the hill, it skirts Swanscoe Hall (this can be see from the brow of Kerridge Road, shortly after the junction with Lidgetts Lane). Immediately, our road bends sharply left – do not go straight on.

The road then meets the main B5470, which goes into Macclesfield.

Section g-h

Turn right into the B5470, which although busy, is not too difficult to join. This road then goes uphill for a short time, but soon begins what for us is a merciful decline towards Macclesfield.

Pass through Higher Hurdsfield, perhaps stopping for refreshment at the George & Dragon on your left, and continue downwards for about half a mile, until you turn right into Hulley Road, which is clearly marked.

This initially goes through a residential area, and past a school, before going into Hurdsfield Industrial Estate. Follow the road right up to the roundabout with the new A523 Macclesfield by-pass. **Note:** if you are using an old map, this may not be marked, so follow these instructions carefully. Also note that the roundabout signs point northwards along the A523 to get to the Middlewood Way. **Do not follow these signs.**

Go straight across the roundabout with the A523, following the signs to Tytherington, and then immediately turn right through a gate onto the Middlewood Way. Although this is not clearly marked, it is obvious, being the first path you come to.

Section h-a

We are now on the home stretch, as we follow the Way north. Due to the new Macclesfield by-pass, riders get an interesting ride over a rather strange bridge, which crosses the road, to take the Way back into Bollington. It is a large arched bridge, and certainly one you wouldn't miss either on it or under it.

The Way continues then as it used to, bringing us right back into Bollington, and our car park at Clough Bank. Now take a well-earned rest!

8. Bollington to Higher Poynton

Distance: 11 miles/17.5km.

Route: Bollington – Poynton – Higher Poynton – Middlewood – Higher Poynton – West Park Gate – Pott Shrigley – Bollington.

Surface: Gravel and Tarmac.

Start: Peaks & Plains Discovery Centre, Grimshaw Lane, Bollington (SJ930775).

Map: O.S. Landranger 109 (Manchester and surrounding area) and O.S. 118 (the Potteries).

The Route

This is based on The Middlewood Way, à reclaimed railway track which starts in Macclesfield and runs through Bollington to Rose Hill in Marple. The Peaks & Plains Discovery Centre, from where we start, is operated by The Groundwork Trust and it often has displays of photographs and materials concerned with either the historical heritage or natural history of the area. The Centre itself is in a stone-built lodge, part of the old Adelphi Mill, now restored to a mini-industrial and leisure complex. The canal is just above the Centre building, so it's worth a look around before you take to the saddle.

There is some car parking around the Discovery Centre, with more in Grimshaw Lane, plus bike hire (but not in the winter) – best to check availability before arriving.

The Journey

Section a-b

Join the Middlewood Way just downhill from The Discovery Centre – be sure to head off in the right direction, signed "Marple 12.2km". The route is shared with both pedestrians and horse riders; since the latter churn up their section, it's usually best to keep to the pedestrian section, whilst giving way to walkers as necessary.

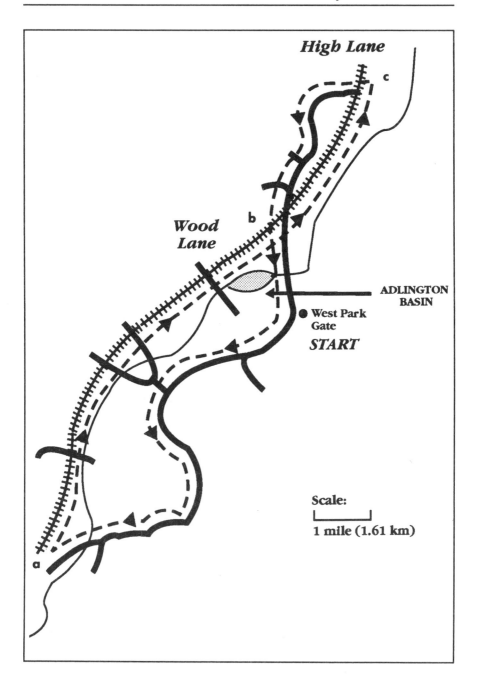

Continue along the route for a little over four miles. Although at first sight bland and never-ending, the route always holds some interest. Careful conservation management (by Macclesfield Borough Council Countryside Rangers) has maintained a rich habitat for wildlife along this old railway track; a series of leaflets is available from The Discovery Centre and other sources. About three miles along, you can make a small diversion to Adlington Basin, where you can admire the canal boats and/or pop into the Miners Arms.

The old platform on The Middlewood Way, at Higher Poynton

After another mile or so, you reach Higher Poynton, with the attractive remnants of a station and refreshments available from either The Boars Head or The Coffee Tavern. From here, you can either:

(A) Continue towards Middlewood, or

(B) Wait for the "A party" to go to Middlewood and meet you here on the way back, or

(C) Go back the way you came.

The extra bit (half a mile or so) is very easy, but there's a steep-ish climb back to Higher Poynton.

Section b-c

Continue along The Way for half a mile or so. Then, leave the cycleway just before a stone-built road-bridge by pushing your bike up the stepped incline (for identification, there is a wooden sign on a bridge pillar labelled "Pool House Road, Marple 4.6km, Macclesfield 11.3km). At the end of the incline, notice the view of "The Cage" in Lyme Park, ahead of you, then turn left over the bridge and along the lane (Pool House Road). Turn left again at the T-junction.

After half a mile, turn left up Anson Road and continue uphill to a crossroads, where you turn right onto Shrigley Road North. This is where you re-join the shorter "B" route.

Section c-a

Carry on with Middlewood Way on your left, then turn left at the next T-junction to cycle along Shrigley Road; cross a bridge and go round a right-hand bend and you'll now see Middlewood Way on your right.

The next mile is an increasingly steep, winding, route relieved on a downhill stretch by "The Coffee Pot" cafe; this was once a "tin tabernacle" chapel-cum-reading-room; note the incongruous Star of David window above the entrance.

At the next T-junction, turn left (signposted "Bollington 2"). There's a few hundred yards of uphill work then a fast downhill stretch. After a little less than a mile, the road bends sharply right at Pott Shrigley – the church here is worth a visit.

Head towards Bollington, but rather than using the main road, take the first fork left along Spuley Lane. You'll pass The Cheshire Hunt and The Country Cafe on the left, then come to a T-junction where you turn right, downhill towards Palmerston Street, in the centre of Bollington. Turn left at the next T-junction and cycle through the town, passing under both its bridges (the canal aqueduct and the old railway viaduct). Turn left again into Grimshaw Lane (opposite the Waggon & Horses) to return to your starting point.

9. Bollington, Kerridge and Rainow

Distance: 7.5 miles/12km.

Route: Bollington – Kerridge – Kerridge End – Brookhouse – Rainow – Ginclough – Bollington.

Surface: Tarmac and gravel.

Start: Middlewood Way car park (SK931779).

Map: O.S. 118 (the Potteries).

The Route

This is a short but steep journey.

The ride winds its way around the ups and downs of Bollington's streets, before climbing towards Cheshire's Peaks and then along the west-facing side of Kerridge Hill before dropping down to meet the B5470.

From here, the ride passes through Rainow and into the Peak National Park. Half a mile along the road, the route takes a left turning before dropping down a very steep hill which before returning to Bollington.

There are numerous pubs and points of refreshment along this route: a dozen or more in Bollington, plus The Rising Sun Inn at Kerridge End, and The Robin Hood at Rainow.

The Journey

Section a-b

Start the ride at the Middlewood Way car park by the viaduct and public toilets. Leave the car park and turn right, following Adlington Road up to the top of the hill and the junction. Turn left at the junction onto Palmerston Road, riding past the Dog & Partridge pub on the left hand side as you go. Continue along Palmerston Road and under the large canal bridge; go through the traffic lights and bear left.

From here, follow the signs for Pott Shrigley. Follow the road ahead up the hill past the Holly Bush on the left and the Meridian on the right-hand side of the road. Go over the crest of the hill and drop down towards the bend which bears left to Pott Shrigley.

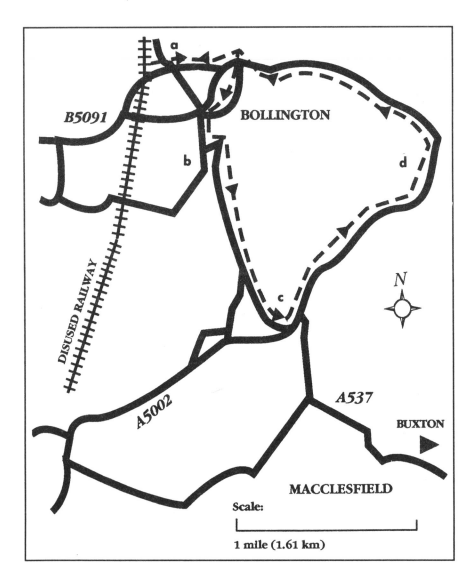

Turn right off this bend onto Church Street, taking great care as you do so. Follow Church Street and pass the Church House Inn on the left and the St John the Baptist Church on the right. Head down the steep hill towards the dye factory and continue around the right hand bend, following the hill before it levels out by the paper factory.

Follow what is now Lord Street up a very steep hill between terraced houses. At the top of Lord Street, Bollington will be in view. Go past the Red Lion on the right and follow the road along a less-steep hill than the previous one. Ride ahead until you meet a junction on a bend. Turn left here onto Jackson Lane, which is part of the Cheshire Cycleway. Ride past the Belgrade Hotel on the right and head up the incline towards the Bulls Head pub on the left-hand side.

Section b-c

At the Bulls Head, turn left into Redway which is still on the Cheshire Cycleway. Climb the hill with high walls on the left and right towards the Redway Tavern. **Note:** if stopping at the Redway Tavern, why not go for a short walk up to the White Nancy monument? This is a viewpoint with panoramic views of the Peak District and Cheshire Plains.

Bollington, from the White Nancy monument

After passing the Redway Tavern, follow the switchback around up the hill and along the edge of Kerridge Hill. A few hundred metres along Redway, the road curves left and levels out. It then passes two quarries – the first is disused.

Ride past what appears to be a castle turret on the right-hand side of the road (this is "Clayton's Chimney" – an intended ventilation shaft for a coal pit; it was probably never used as a chimney, and its decorative appearance may have been an attempt to make it more acceptable). Drop down slightly and ride up a gentle hill with cottages on the left. Continue along what is now Windmill Lane onto Kerridge Road with Macclesfield in view on the right.

Before Windmill Lane drops downhill, take the first turning left into Lidgetts Lane which is clearly signposted with a Cheshire Cycleway sign.

Follow the narrow lane up the hill towards Rainow. The route goes past an electricity sub-station before dropping down a very steep hill. **Note:** 50 yards before the end of the hill, the road makes a sharp left turn before the junction. **Take care on this section.**

At the junction, turn left off Lidgetts Lane onto the B5470, again following the Cheshire Cycleway sign as you go.

Section c-d

Ride down the hill along Hawkins Lane into Kerridge End past the Rising Sun Inn and go down the 1-in-9 hill towards the centre of Rainow.

Go over the River Dean at the base of the hill and up the other side of Pedley Hill, passing Holy Trinity Church on the right. Follow the road ahead onto what is now Church Lane. Ride up the hill through Rainow with the Robin Hood pub on the left. Immediately after the pub you cross the boundary into the Peak National Park. Follow the road ahead out of Rainow. Just before entering the tiny hamlet of Ginclough, the hill levels out. The road then bends sharply left and climbs once more. At the crest of the hill, drop down for a few hundred metres before leaving the B5470 and following signs for Bollington which is a mile and a half away.

Section d-a

This section of the ride is undoubtedly the steepest, fastest and most dangerous of all hills on the route. At $1^1/_2$ miles in length it would be very wise to make sure that brakes are in full working order.

Follow the hill towards Bollington until reaching the "Poacher" on the left of the bend which curves right. Continue heading downhill to a junction opposite the bend you left earlier. Turn into Church Street and, before reaching the junction, note the Cotton Tree pub on the left and the toilets opposite.

Cross the junction onto the bend and follow the road ahead into Bollington. Head down the hill, go through the traffic lights and under the canal once again.

Ride along Palmerston Street before reaching the Dog & Partridge on the right. Turn right into Adlington Road and continue to the Middlewood Way car park.

10. Chelford, Siddington and Nether Alderley

Distance: 13.5 miles/22km.

Route: Chelford Station – Siddington – A537 near Birtles – Nether Alderley – A34 – Chelford.

Surface: Tarmac, gravel, hard-core, cobbles.

Start: Chelford Station (SJ814749).

Map: O.S. 118 (the Potteries).

The Route

If you fancy a gentle, pleasant ride through the rolling Cheshire countryside, then this could be the one for you. It travels close to Nether Alderley Mill, an Elizabethan corn mill and past Redesmere, a pleasant lake with ducks, swans and often dinghies from the local sailing club. It is by no means an off-road route, but some rough tracks mean that it's not the best choice for your best lightweight road-bike.

Refreshments are no problem, with a couple of grocers and newsagents in Chelford, as well as the Dixon Arms Hotel and the Simply Steaks Restaurant. There's also the Egerton Arms just outside Chelford.

Note: Although major A-roads are avoided as much as possible it is sometimes necessary to follow them for short distances, and where this occurs they can be quite busy and fast moving. However, there are footpaths along these roads and well, it is the countryside and there aren't that many pedestrians . . . just be careful and remember to give way.

The Journey

a-b

Depending on how you arrived at Chelford station, you could be on either side of the railway track.

If you have arrived from the Manchester direction:

- go up the narrow footpath to the left leading up to the A537 and turn left over the railway bridge.

If you arrived from the Crewe direction by train:

- make your way off the platform into the car park where obviously you would find yourself if you had arrived by car.

Ride out of the car park and turn left, up and over the railway bridge. Here the two routes converge and follow the A537 down to a large roundabout, a distance of around 400 metres.

At the roundabout take the A535 signposted Holmes Chapel and Birmingham M6; this is 270 degrees to the right. Follow this down the hill and past St John the Evangelist Church on the left. The road curves around to the right and climbs up slightly. Take the first turn on the left, Congleton Lane, about 400 metres from the roundabout.

This road is followed for about 4.5 km. You pass Chapel Wood to your left, Mill Lane around 2 km down on your left, and Piggot Hill Farm on the right, just after which the road changes from Congleton Lane to Chelford Road. Follow the road through the 90 degree right-hand bend, just after a track to Blake House Farm on your left and Slable Cottage on your right. The road curls around to the left and Whisterfield Lane merges from the right as you come into the village of Siddington. You pass the police station on your left and a phone box before you arrive at. a T-junction. Bear left (almost straight on) signposted to Macclesfield. After a couple of hundred metres you arrive at a staggered crossroads with the A34. Right is signposted to Congleton, left is signposted to Manchester. Straight across to the left is the B5392.

Section b-c

Go left and cycle along the A34 towards Manchester, the road climbs slightly and you take the next right after the B5392. The road you want

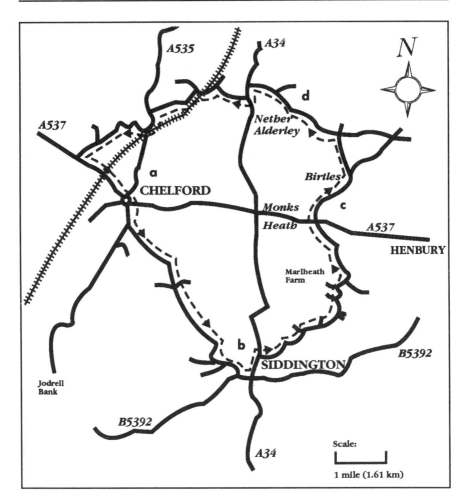

is Fanshawe Lane, opposite a small post box and signposted 'Henbury 3'. Cycle down this and on your left, after around 200 metres, is Redesmere. There are usually plenty of ducks and swans around, and often dinghies from the local sailing club, on the opposite side of the water. There is space to park cars on the right-hand side and, if you are lucky, an ice cream van.

Follow the road away from the lake as it starts to rise, with farms on the left and right. Keep cycling as the road twists and undulates; on the left you pass a large cream-coloured sign for Marlheath Farm after around 2 km. The road levels off, bends right and then drops downhill. You want the next road on the left, signposted to Chelford (the sign may be partially obscured by foliage), opposite a short row of cottages, around 100 metres down from the Marlheath sign. Follow this down and then up with woods on the right. The road levels off and drops down quite sharply, curving to the left. Don't go too quickly here as just around the corner is a cross roads with the fast moving A537.

Section c-d

Go straight across at the crossroads, signposted 'Birtles and Over Alderley'. This is Birtles Lane. Ride along the lane and, as it starts to gently climb, Birtles Hall can be seen across the fields to the left. Keep going, past St. Catherine's Church (quite small and easy to miss) on the left about a kilometre from the crossroads.

Just beyond the church on the left, opposite a cottage on the right, is a tarmac-surfaced track through a stone wall, with 'Higher Bark Farm' engraved into it. Follow this over the cattle grid (it may be necessary to dismount) and continue over the second cattle grid and up towards the farm.

Approaching the farm, the track splits three ways. Take the left fork up to a gate. Proceed through the gate, past the house on the left and along the track which deteriorates from tarmac to a stony surface.

After a short distance, the route becomes a gravel drive for the recently-developed Jarman's Farm on the left. Shortly after this, you arrive at a staggered crossroads.

Go left down the cobbled track (a RUPP – "road used as a public path"). Pass Acton Farm on the right and after a few hundred metres from the crossroads, the track becomes metalled, with houses on the right. To the left you can see across the tree-tops of the Cheshire plain. As you continue, the road degrades to a hard-core surface, with a few pot-holes that can easily be dodged. Keep riding along this bridleway, past Haymans House to the right. The road smooths out and drops down through a wooded section with a few speed bumps. Continue through the gateway past a beautiful stone cottage to the right, a few hundred metres on.

Carry straight on to a fork in the road with a sign on the right proclaiming it to be a bridleway with no access to cars. Go left down the cobbled track past the houses on the left. Follow this for just over half a kilometre, past Nether Alderley School on the right, and down to a T-junction with the A34, with a phone box on the left.

Section d-a

Turn left onto the A34 and follow it past cottages on the right. Take the first right, 'Sand Lane', signposted 'Warford 2'. Be careful here, however, as the A34 bends round to the left and it may be hard to see oncoming cars.

NOTE: Nether Alderley Mill is about 100 yards further along the A34, past Sand Lane. Owned by the National Trust, it is an Elizabethan water powered corn mill, restored to working power and now producing flour. It's open between April and October, Sundays, Wednesdays and Bank Holidays; between July and September, every day except Monday. You have to pay to get in unless you are a member of the National Trust.

Nether Alderley Mill

Cycle along Sand Lane, past the big houses on the right. The road bends to the left and you come to a T-junction. Take a left turn, and follow the road round, over the railway bridge. As you drop down from this, take the first left, signposted 'Chelford', running parallel to the railway. Cycle along this as it bends around to the right and passes a house on the left. Keep cycling until you reach a T-junction. The road you meet is the A535, along which you go left, again signposted 'Chelford'.

Ride down the road and over a small bridge. The road bends right and approaches a railway bridge with traffic lights. Just before the lights there is a hard-core track off to the right to 'Fir Tree Farm'. Take this track (another RUPP) and follow it past Fir Tree Cottage on the right, with woods on the left. Keep cycling, with open fields on the left and right, and you'll see the farm straight ahead. The top of Jodrell Bank's dish can be seen above the trees, roughly 55 degrees to the left of the track's direction.

As you arrive at the farm itself, the track bears right into the farmyard. A narrow path goes straight ahead to the left of the farm and a fence that juts out from it. Cycle along this and after a few metres, the track emerges from the farmyard on the right. Head straight on down the track, away from the farm, passing a cottage to the right. Follow the track for about a third of a kilometre, where you emerge at a junction at the back of a modern housing development. Opposite is a green sign saying 'Carter Lane 1+2'. On the right is a sign saying 'Carter Lane.'

Turn left into the estate, onto the tarmac road. Follow the second right, the main road going through the estate, past a small park on the left, and up to a give-way sign at a crossroads with the A537. To the right is the Egerton Arms, a Chef and Brewer pub with a small beer garden around the back.

To get back to Chelford, turn left out of Dixon Drive, onto the A537. This will take you the few hundred metres into Chelford, with the Station on the far side of town, down a road to the left, just before the railway bridge.

11. Chelford and The Peovers

Distance: 13 miles/21km.

Route: Chelford – Over Peover – Lower Peover – Chelford.

Surface: Tarmac and short sections of sometimes muddy bridleways.

Start: Chelford Station (SJ814749) or, if you have a car, park in the layby on the A535 or at other parking spots on this road.

Map: O.S. 118 (the Potteries).

The Route

There's scarcely a hill on this ride, but plenty of interest. Apart from two short stretches of main road and a slightly awkward junction, this one is ideal for a family and even has a muddy stretch for the more adventurous (mum and dad can walk this bit). There are several pubs, some interesting churches and even Jodrell Bank Radio Telescope, a fascinating and educational visit towards the end of the journey.

If arriving by train, use Chelford Station, then cycle the short distance (south east) to the major roundabout to join the route. If you have the bike with your car, park on the first layby on the A535 south of the roundabout – or at one of the other parking spots on this road.

The Journey

Section a-b

Begin by heading north, towards Chelford, and take the second exit from the roundabout, to pass Chelford Cricket Club. Follow this road for a couple of miles, crossing the railway and then coming to a T-junction. Turn right here, then first left into Over Peover.

The road continues through the village passing "The Dog" public house on your right (previously "The Gay Dog", but sensitivities changed that!). Turn left at the crossroads (Over Peover School as a landmark), and head down Clay Lane. Go over a staggered crossroads and, after a

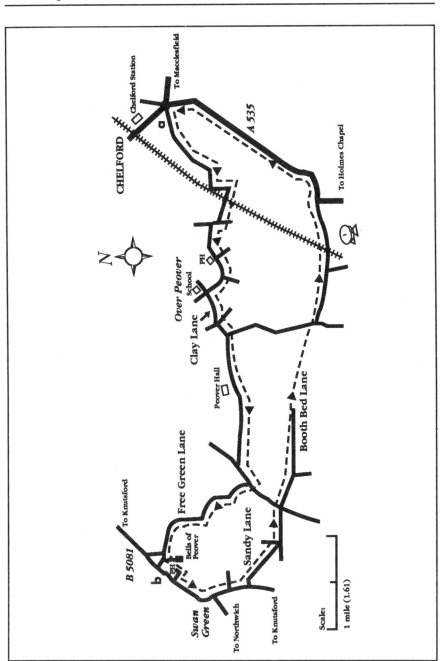

short distance, where the road bends left, you turn right along a tarmac bridleway. Soon, on your right, you see Peover Hall and its nearby church.

The tarmac peters out at a couple of cottages. Go straight on here, through a gateway – do not turn right along what might look like the obvious track. Soon, you are cycling along what seems more like a footpath (it really *is* a bridleway) which eventually becomes a smoother-surfaced track.

At the end of this lane (appropriately called Long Lane) turn left onto a busy main road and then first right. *Note: This is a dangerous turn – it may be best to dismount.*

This road, Free Green Lane, takes you to Lower Peover. Ignore left turns until, where the road forks right to Broome Lane, keep left along Free Green Lane. Turn left down Barrows Brow. Follow the track round to the Bells of Peover public house, pausing for a welcome break. You can visit nearby St Oswald's Church for spiritual refreshment, too.

Section b-a

Ride out to the main road, turn left and continue south. Take the second turn left into Sandy Lane. At a junction, take the second left turn, into Town Field Lane passing immediately a farm on the right. Carry on to a crossroads and go straight over. Continue in the same (easterly) direction along Booth Bed Lane.

At a junction, fork left, despite the "No Through Road" warning. After almost a mile, proceed along a rough track ignoring the "Private Road" warning – it's a public bridleway.

After a somewhat bumpy ride, where the track curves right into a farm yard, continue straight ahead along a muddier track and through a wood. This is most easily tackled with a mountain bike, but you can do it on a tourer – with the occasional dismounting for the muddiest areas!

At the end of the bridleway, turn right along the road, then left – signposted to Withington Green. Further along this lane you get some super views of one of Jodrell Bank's radio telescopes and you pass the public entrance - ideal for some scientific enlightenment on the route.

At the end of the lane, bear left and, at the main road, turn left on to the busy A535, returning to your starting point. (If you really have to avoid the A535, consult your OS Map and follow the lanes back through Batemill, to Peover Heath and along the lane past Chelford Cricket Club, which is also convenient for the station.

The Lovell Radio telescope at Jodrell Bank
(by permission, Jodrell Bank, Nuffield Radio Astronomy Laboratories,
University of Manchester)

12. Chester to Wales, and back!

Distance: 21 miles/34km.

Route: Chester Railway Station – Lache – Balderton – Dodleston – Gorstella – Lower Kinnerton – Higher Kinnerton – Burton – Pulford – Eccleston – Chester Town centre – Chester Railway Station.

Surface: Tarmac.

Start: Chester Railway Station (SK413670).

Map: O.S. 117 (Chester).

The Route

The route starts from Chester Railway Station but other landmarks for starting points include Chester Cathedral or one of the tourist information centres in the city centre. This ride leaves the historic walls of Chester and heads south over the River Dee towards Wales. From the Welsh border, it winds along quiet country lanes just north of Wrexham until heading back north into England. We make a bee-line along a Roman road back to Chester, passing through the pretty village of Eccleston.

There are plenty of refreshment stops, including The Bear & Billet, Lower Bridge Street, Chester, the Golden Grove Inn just outside Burton and The Grosvenor Arms at Pulford.

The Journey

Section a-b

There is a mini-roundabout directly in front of the station entrance. Ride across this and follow the signs for the town centre. Cross over the River Dee and continue to a junction. Turn left here and ride up to the traffic lights, following the signs for the City centre and North Wales. Ride past the Telegraph Petrol Station on the right and follow Grosvenor Park Road round the bend to the right.

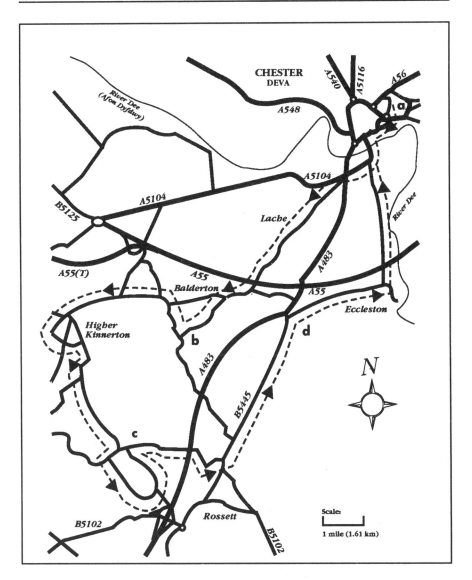

From here, bear left following the sign to North Wales, painted on the road. The Tourist Information office is on the right as the road curves left towards the traffic lights. Ride through the lights and under the City Walls, into Little St John Street.

A few hundred metres along, turn left into Lower Bridge Street and drop down the hill, under the City Walls and once again over the River Dee.

Bear right at all times and ride up the hill past St Mary's Parish church. Follow the road ahead to a triangular-shaped roundabout. Take the second exit down Lache Lane. The route leaves the suburbs of Chester and heads towards the Welsh hills.

Ride under the A55(T), follow the bend right and ride over the level crossing. Before reaching Balderton, take the first left for Dodleston and follow the quiet country lane into the village.

Section b-c

On entering Dodleston take the first right up Kinnerton Road, immediately after Dodleston Primary School. Follow this road along as it winds around the Cheshire/Wales borderlands. At the end of Kinnerton Road, turn left and continue along the road towards Lower Kinnerton, three-quarters of a mile away.

Bear left at all times along this stretch. Ride through Lower Kinnerton and follow the bend around to the left. Just after the bend, the route crosses the England/Wales border into Clwyd.

Ride past the Royal Oak pub as you enter Higher Kinnerton and continue along Main Road towards Hope. Opposite Higher Kinnerton's Church is Bennetts Lane. Turn left here and drop down the hill until reaching a junction at Kinnerton Green.

Turn right onto the Green. Ride over Brad Brook and follow the lane ahead as it curves right and then sharply left. Continue along the lane until the junction at Burton Green. Turn right towards Caer Gwrle. Ride along this lane until you arrive upon the first lane on the left. Turn left here, following the signs for Burton.

Section c-d

Ride into Burton and take a sharp left bend before arriving in the centre of the village. At the junction, turn left off Rosemary Hall Lane onto Burton Hall Road. Follow this road to another junction a mile down the road. Turn right here towards Pulford.

A mile down the road, ride over the A483 and drop down over the level crossing, taking care as you go. The road then takes a sharp right. Follow this road along for a few hundred metres, turn first left and continue, following the signs for Pulford and Chester. Ride along a short distance to a junction. Turn left here onto the B5445 away from Rossett and follow the road back into England and Cheshire. After about two miles, pass through Pulford and, just before a large roundabout, take the first right into Rake Lane.

Section d-a

Ride ahead towards Eccleston along Rake Lane. After entering Eccleston, drop down the hill and take the second road on the left for Chester. This long and straight road was originally Roman.

Once again, ride over the A55(T); the River Dee is on the right-hand side. Continue through Chester's suburbs until reaching a junction. Turn right here, back onto the road from where the route started. Drop down the hill, over the River Dee and under the City Walls. Follow Lower Bridge Street and, at the traffic lights turn right and follow the road past the Visitor Centre on the left. The station is well-signed from here.

The Groves, River Dee (by permission, Chester City Council)

13. Chester and Christleton

Distance: 23 miles/37km.

Route: Chester – Pipers Ash – Littleton – Christleton – Waverton – Higher Huxley Hall – Bruera – Aldford – Chester

Surface: Tarmac.

Start: Chester Railway Station (SK413670).

Map: O.S. 117 (Chester).

The Route

Starting at Chester Railway Station, we head east towards Littleton and Christleton, then south east along the Cheshire Cycleway, parallel to the Shropshire Union Canal. The ride heads west across the A41 to Bruera and onwards to circle the small village of Aldford. From here, the route joins the B5130 and heads north back to Chester.

For refreshments, try the Rake & Pickle or the Red Horse, both in Chester.

The Journey

Section a-b

From the station entrance, turn right and follow Brook Street to the traffic lights. Turn right and ride over the railway bridge. Drop down and turn right into Lightfoot Street. At a mini-roundabout, ride straight ahead to a junction. Turn left here onto Hoole Lane. Continue along Hoole Lane over a second mini-roundabout towards the A41(T). At this point, dismount and cross the main road. At Guilden Sutton Lane (immediately after the A41) turn left into Hare Lane.

Ride over the railway line and away from Piper's Ash. The road crosses the M53 motorway. Half a mile from the beginning of Hare Lane, cross the junction of the A51 into Littleton and ride down Littleton Lane towards Christleton.

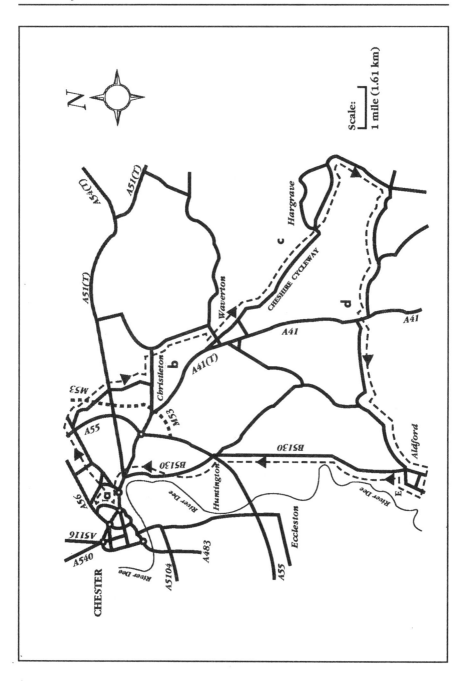

Section b-c

In the centre of Christleton, take the first left into Birch Heath Lane. Continue east out of the village until meeting the end of Birch Heath Lane, where you turn right onto Rake Lane (part of the 135 mile Cheshire Cycleway).

Ride on to Waverton. At the junction, turn right and follow signs for Chester. Follow the road over the Shropshire Union Canal and drop down towards the crossroads. At the crossroads, turn left, following the Cheshire Cycleway signs.

Ride along Common Lane out of Waverton and parallel to the Shropshire Union Canal. Two miles down Common Lane the road curves sharply left and narrows as it crosses the Shropshire Union Canal. After the hump-backed bridge, drop down and bear right.

Section c-d

Follow the road ahead past Higher Huxley hall on the right and around the right-hand bend. Ride over the Shropshire Union Canal once again and then over the railway line.

At the crossroads, turn right towards Gatesheath. Follow the lane, over the disused rail line and, at the junction, turn right and follow the signs for Chester. Follow the lane ahead to the A41(T). Turn right here continuing along the A41 for only a short distance before taking the first left towards Bruera.

Section d-e

After the left turn, ride around a sharp right and then a left bend before reaching the centre of Bruera. At the junction turn left and follow the signs for Aldford a mile and a quarter away.

Give way on the sharp bend. Ride on over Aldford brook and bear left, following signs for Wrexham along the B5130. Continue for about 300 metres before turning right down Rushmere Lane. Ride along this lane and turn right onto School Lane; this becomes Church Lane and St John the Baptist Church will be on the left.

Eastgate Clock (by permission, Chester City Council)

Section e-a

Continue along Church Lane to the B5130. Turn left here and again ride over Aldford Brook. Ride around the bend as it curves left and follow the route ahead.

Ride under an iron bridge and continue back towards Chester. Ride over the A55(T) and enter the Chester suburb of Huntington. Ride up the hill to a junction and the end of the B5130. Turn left here and head back to the city centre. At the square-shaped round-about, take the third exit back to the station.

14. Chester and its Zoo!

Distance: 17 miles/27km.

Route: Chester – Chester Zoo – Croughton – Picton – Guilden Sutton – Chester

Surface: Tarmac

Start: Safeway Carpark, Bache (next to Bache Station) (SK405683). There may be parking restrictions at this car park, so check before leaving a car here.

Map: O.S. 117 (Chester).

The Route

This ride passes within a stone's throw of Chester Zoo, which you may want to visit. The route then wends its way through the West Cheshire countryside, returning to its starting point, on the outskirts of the historic Roman city of Chester. There are several pubs on the route, some serving food as well as drink, plus the Safeway store at Bache, open 7 days a week.

The Journey

Section a-b

Drop downhill out of Safeway's car park and turn right, under the railway bridge and ride uphill through a residential area. At the crossroads, go straight over and follow signs for Chester Zoo. You pass the Wheatsheaf pub on the right and go through a set of traffic lights. Soon after the crossroads, a green mesh fence on the left borders the zoo.

If you are visiting the zoo, ride into the car park. Speak to an attendant near the entrance, and find a safe place to leave your (locked) bicycle. Otherwise, turn left down a lane immediately after the zoo entrance. (If you are coming out of the zoo, simply go left and you will be on the correct road, just 200-300 yards further on.) Follow the road through a

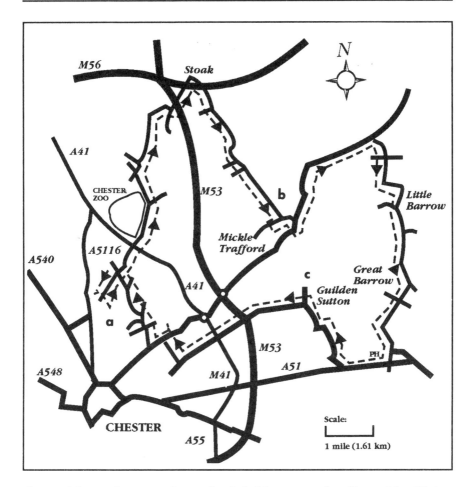

sharp right and over a hump-back bridge over the Shropshire Union Canal – keep straight, don't go left. The road twists along and, soon, you can see the oil refineries at Ellesmere Port to the right, about a mile and a half away.

Go into Croughton, and drop down into a little hamlet, past Pennywell Farm on the right. The road curves right, and you cross the canal again and approach a T-junction. Go left here, following signs for Stoak and Little Stanney. Cycle under the M53, and follow the road around to the right, passing under the M56. The road bears left, but you ride right, up to the junction. Follow signs for Picton and Mickle Trafford, down to the right and over the motorway.

Keep following the road ahead as it twists and turns – Delamere Forest can be seen across the plain ahead. Continue pedalling and follow the road into Picton.

Cycle past Manor Farm, spanning both sides of the road, and drop downhill and around to the right. Pass Mickleton Farm on the right and Mickle Trafford water works a little further on, on the left. At the T-junction, at the end of Picton lane, turn left and head into Mickle Trafford.

Section b-c

Ride along the road through the estate and up to a T-junction, where you turn left. This is the A56, part of the Cheshire cycleway. (There are paths on both sides of the road if necessary.) You pass Deeside sawmills on the left and, further on, the Shrewsbury Arms on the left, as you progress into Bridge Trafford. Cross a bridge over the River Gowy and, on the left, the Nags Head pub and restaurant.

Keep going for around another half mile or so until you pass Lofty's garage on the left, and cycle over a railway bridge. Take the second right, the B5132, signed to Barrow and Stamford Bridge. Go straight across the crossroads to Little Barrow and Great Barrow. As you come to the top of the hill, the Foxcote Inn is a welcome sight on the left.

Pass through Great Barrow and head straight for Stamford Bridge and Tarvin. The road drops downhill and through a sharp left; continue all the way up to a T-junction with traffic lights, where the B5132 meets the A51. Turn right, signposted to North Wales and Chester. The A51 is quite wide and fast flowing; if necessary, there is a footpath on the right.

Take the first turn to the right, Wicker Lane, to Guilden Sutton and Mickle Trafford, about a kilometre down the road from the traffic lights. Continue into Guilden Sutton, a town with newly-developed housing.

Section c-a

The road drops down to the left. Take the second road on the left, School Lane, to Chester. This is a tree-lined road with a high wall on the right leading towards Pipers Ash. Ride over the railway, under the M53, up the other side and past terraced houses on the left.

At a T-junction with the A41, go straight across; you are strongly advised to walk your bike across this fast road, though there is a central refuge.

Ride along Hoole lane until you come to a mini-roundabout, where you go right into Canadian Avenue. Continue to a T-junction with the A56. Go left here, then take the first road of any note on the right, just before the traffic lights. Follow this over the narrow railway bridge; take the third left, Wealstone Lane.

You pass a Primary School then Upton library, and continue to the junction with Heath Road; go left here, following signs to Bache station, half a mile away. The road becomes Mill Lane, and drops downhill towards the station. Pass under the railway bridge and the Safeway carpark is on your left.

15. Congleton: Astbury and Mow Cop

Distance: 11 miles/17.5km.

Route: Astbury – Scholar Green – Mow Cop – Astbury.

Surface: Tarmac and Grass.

Start: Astbury Church (SJ846616).

Map: O.S. 118 (the Potteries).

The Route

This short ride uses quiet lanes on level ground to the south of Congleton before a short, sharp climb to geologically and historically significant Mow Cop (335m). From here it runs at a more gradual pace along the Staffordshire Way and back to the start point at Astbury Church.

A short diversion of a mile from Scholar Green (southern most point of the ride would take you to the exceedingly good tea rooms of Little Moreton Hall (National Trust). The tea rooms at Astbury itself can be recommended as can the Egerton Arms opposite Astbury church.

The ride probably offers more views per mile pedalled than most and can be accomplished comfortably within an hour and a half.

The Journey

Section a-b

Leaving Astbury Church behind, you turn left onto the A34. Continue for half a mile before turning right down Childs Lane and then left down a wide grassy track. At Ivy Cottage turn right and continue to T-junction. Ignore the turn to the left which leads back onto the busy A34 and turn instead to the right following the Cheshire Cycle-Way sign.

Continue for two miles to T-junction opposite Rode Pool, concealed behind a screen of trees. Turn left this time ignoring the Cheshire

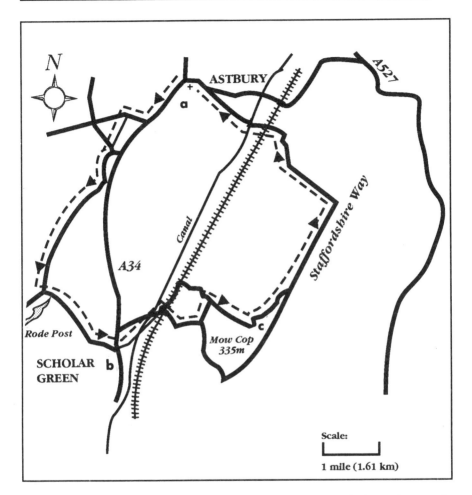

Cycle-Way sign. Mow Cop, the literal high point of the ride stands proud on the skyline to the left. Pass All Saints Church on the left (work of the famous Victorian Gothic architect Sir George Gilbert Scott) and Rode Hall and Gardens (open to the public on a seasonal basis) on the right and continue to the junction with Congleton Road North at Scholar Green. Turn left.

Note: To visit Little Moreton Hall continue north on the A34 for a mile. The Hall is on the right.

Little Moreton Hall (Chris Rushton)

Turn first right down the one-way Cinderhill Lane running parallel to the canal. Turn right at a T-junction past the Three Horseshoes Pub, passing the Rising Sun and going over the canal. Bear right under the railway to climb Spring Bank. Where the road swings round a right-angle bend to the right, turn left into Birch Tree Lane. At the end, turn right and climb steep (10%) Station Road into steeper (1:4, 25%) Top Station Road to Mow Cop. Turn left.

Section b-c

Note: Mow Cop is a maze of pathways and little streets. If you suspect you're lost just go up until you see the folly and, having arrived, head left (north east) aiming for the radio mast to leave Mow Cop along the spine of the hill. Only one road leads out of the village this way, so you'd be hard put to miss it!

On reaching the top, leave your bike by the National Trust Information Board; read it, and scramble up to the folly to catch your breath and marvel at the view.

Note: The folly was built in 1754 to give Randle Wilbraham of Rode Hall, three miles away, a more interesting skyline to look at. Geologically the hill (millstone grit and sandstone) is a continuation of The Cloud. Coal was quarried on the east side and limestone on the west. The site is famous locally as the venue for an open air Methodist meeting of 1807 at which a return to primitive Methodism was established. Indeed it is hard to move anywhere in the roads leading to Mow Cop without encountering a Methodist Chapel.

Section c-a

Return to the High Street from the folly and turn right. Continue to the end and turn right into Wood Lane, over the top by the radio mast and drop down to join the Staffordshire Way at Mow Cop Inn.

Note: To the left of the radio mast a footpath leads to the Old Man of Mow – a jagged monolithic structure which dominates the skyline seen from the plain.

Turn left and enjoy the freewheel down to Cheshire Close viewpoint and on to the beginning of a well-worn footpath leading to Congleton Edge. You may wish to pause and exercise some walking muscles here. If not, follow the road which sweeps away to the left, steeply. Pass the Horseshoe Pub, turn left over the railway line (ignoring the alternative route to Astbury for heavy vehicles) and canal. At the give-way sign, turn left into Peel Lane. This brings you back to Astbury Church.

Note: The church, which is rarely open during the week, is well worth a visit for its late 15th century stonework and wood-carving. The interior is elegant and utterly peaceful. The setting is further enhanced in Springtime with a beautiful display of daffodils outside the church (see picture with ride 17).

16. Congleton and The Cloud

Distance: 8 miles/12km

Route: Congleton – Timbersbrook – Cloud Side – Congleton.

Surface: Tarmac and Gravel.

Start: Congleton Railway Station (SJ873624).

Map: O.S. 118 (the Potteries).

The Route

This short ride rises to the challenge of the hillier terrain of The Cloud on the Cheshire – Staffordshire border. The area is rich in bilberries, blackberries, heather and dry-stone walls. As a late Summer/early Autumn ride it is unsurpassed. In Winter, when the stone walls outline fields of snow in a Mondrian-like manner, it has a charm all its own.

The route encircles the Cloud gradually, following contours to give a sense of height and achievement for very little effort, and providing pleasing views over the Cheshire plain to the West and Croker Hill, Wildboarclough and Shutlingsloe to the North East.

The start and finish point is Congleton Railway Station where parking may, apparently, be had for free. There are two pubs opposite the station (the Railway Inn and the Green Man), otherwise the route is not well supplied with hostelries. At Timbersbrook, approximately half-way round the route, there is a picnic area with car parking and toilet facilities.

Save for the initial mile necessary to get onto the bridleway the route is quiet and can easily be accomplished within 1 and 2 hours.

The Journey

Section a-b

On leaving the station there are two choices:

Option 1: strictly speaking, you need a permit from British Waterways to cycle along a towpath. So, presuming you've got one, – turn left onto the A527 and take the first left, signposted "Morleys", into the back yard of Morley Daniels (fruit dryers). Immediately across the canal bridge on the right are blue railings marking steps to the tow path. They are not steep, but are narrow. The really determined can man-handle a bike down here and enjoy a mile of peaceful pedalling before leaving the canal at the third bridge (including the one just crossed) and turning right onto the bridleway. At this point the route converges with Option 2.

Option 2: turn right and follow the A527 downhill to the traffic lights. Turn right into Bromley Road (not named at this end) with the phone box and Lawton House Surgery on your left. Continue past Bromley Road Post Office and onto the bridleway, after crossing the railway line.

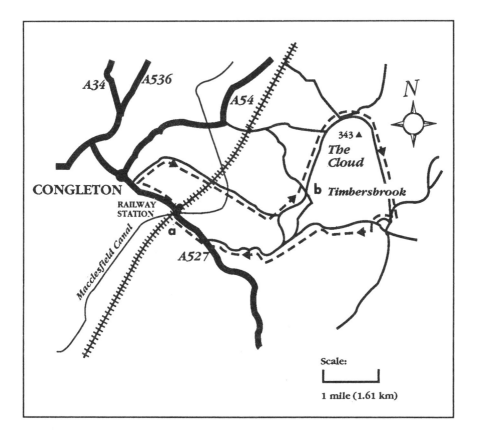

The road descends quickly into Bath Vale to cross a brook and rises again on a broken tarmac and gravel surface past a row of terraced houses on the left. Climb out of this valley, following the bridleway under two railway bridges. The first is the Manchester – London, via Congleton, line, the second, disused. Between the two lies a tranquil pool where a few fish swim and pond skaters and dragonflies skim the surface.

Continue out into the sunlight and follow the bridleway as it crosses the canal. To the right, Mow Cop can be seen (focus of the previous Congleton ride which makes a similar foray into North Staffordshire. To your right, the Cloud, goal of today's endeavour, slumbers artfully.

Continue past the elegant, stone-built Brook House and attendant buildings, following Brook House Lane to its junction with the main road. Turn left and follow the contour-hugging road to Timbersbrook. Note, in passing, Spring Bank Farm's attempt in topiary to transform a Hawthorn bush into a bird.

At Timbersbrook a left turn into Weathercock Lane will take you to Timbersbrook Picnic Area (car park and toilets).

Section b-a

Continue straight ahead and over small crossroads with Acorn Lane to the left and Gosberry Lane to the right. The road climbs to follow a contour of approximately 200m.

To the left a cluster of man's scars on the landscape sidle past: a huge sand quarry, ICI Pharmaceuticals, Alderley Park and Jodrell Bank. The Manchester – London line breaks cover in more-graceful guise as the Congleton viaduct.

Continue to the crossroads where Peover Road joins Tunstall Road. On the left is a group of stately beeches, on the right, a National Trust sign marking the steep footpath which scales the head of the Cloud to the summit at 343m. Our route is more subtle. Turn right and continue round the head of the Cloud, pausing to marvel at its rugged profile, and covering of inaccessible bilberries. Continue over the (unmarked) Staffordshire border, which cleaves the Cloud in two along its length, and round to Cloud Side.

Beyond the turning to Woodhouse Green on the left is Willowshaw Farm, named on the map but otherwise identifiable by the warning "Beware of the Dog". Turn right here and continue until this short road meets the Leek-Congleton road at a T-junction. The climbing is over.

Turn right and descent until the road dips under the disused railway line at Dane in Shaw. BEWARE of the steep 1:7 descent. At traffic lights turn right onto A527 for half a mile and you will be back at the start point.

17. Congleton, Astbury and Swettenham

Distance: 20 Miles/32km.

Route: Congleton – Astbury – Brookhouse Green – Brereton Green – Brereton Heath – Swettenham – Marton – Hulme Walfield – Congleton.

Surface: Tarmac & Gravel.

Start: Congleton Railway Station (SJ873624).

Map: O.S. 118 (the Potteries).

The Route

Winding its way through the leafy lanes at the heart of the Cheshire Plain, this gentle ride offers very little to tax even the most casual cyclist and, indeed, only takes two to four hours to cover the distance. However, for those still seeking an excuse to spend some time out of the saddle, or to explore rather than to sail along, hours more could be easily swallowed up. This makes the route just as ideal as for those who want nothing more than the simpler virtues of beautiful countryside, picturesque villages and striking scenery.

The journey takes in two churches of national renown, and a further two at least worthy of a brief look; a sixteenth century hall; two of the county's most charming villages; a country park and any number of welcoming hostelries. Be sure to carry a puncture repair kit! The combination of a route sticking largely to narrow lanes and the regular need for hedge-cutting, together with the use of bridleways, means there'll be the occasional unfortunate incident, but if you're appropriately prepared, even this shouldn't spoil your ride.

The Journey

Section a-b

This circular route takes as its starting point, simply for ease of access, Congleton Railway Station. However, those who are not arriving by

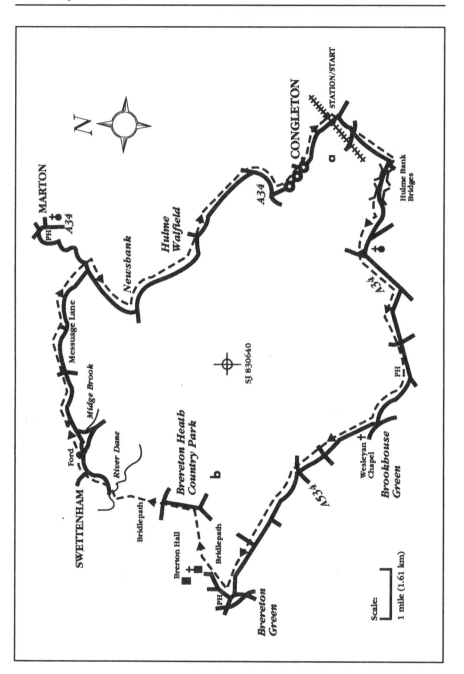

train and who wish to avoid the route's only climb could simply follow the A34 through Congleton and rejoin the route at Astbury by starting elsewhere. There are car parks at Brereton Green, Brereton Heath, Swettenham and Marton.

As you come out of the BR car park, turn left and cross the railway bridge, then taking an immediate right in order to head for the fresh air and scenery of the Cheshire countryside. Turn right at the T-junction you soon reach and then, following the signs to Astbury, taking in as you do so the imposing Bosley Cloud rising up to your left, and as you progress, the castle folly at Mow Cop further to the south. The lane to Astbury crosses both the railway and the Macclesfield Canal by means of narrow humpback bridges where the view of the road ahead is almost completely obscured, so proceed with care.

Astbury Church

This brings you to Astbury, a scene lifted straight off the lid of a chocolate box right down to the village green, ivy clad cottages and a village store that the Famous Five wouldn't look out of place in. The village is dominated by St Mary's, a sizeable stone church which dates largely from the fifteenth century – a mere stripling when set alongside its ancient yew tree. Its interior is similarly impressive, boasting among its delights a beautifully carved ceiling and a rood screen almost as old as the present building. Little wonder that until comparatively recently its now by far larger neighbour, Congleton, was part of St Mary's parish.

Continuing the journey, turn left onto the A34 and pass the sizeable Astbury Meadow Garden Centre before turning right to head for Smallwood. Cycle along this lane, past the commercial greenhouses, only forking right soon after passing the all too inviting Blue Bell Inn. This swiftly brings you to the hamlet of Brookhouse Green whereupon you should turn right just before, and then left immediately after, the Wesleyan chapel. Follow this lane for three miles of comfortable cycling, taking care when crossing the busy A534, until a Post Office signifies that you have reached Brereton Green. Shortly after this, a right turn needs to be made to bring you to another set of picturesque cottages. The village's most notable feature is the Bear's Head – a black and white timbered inn complete with a very literal pub sign!

Before reaching this, you will have passed on your right a striking gatehouse, through which you should now pass – although not signposted as such, this is a public right of way. Fork right and cycle down the hill into the valley of the River Croco, to be rewarded with a view of Brereton Hall and the adjacent church. Built in the days of Queen Elizabeth, the hall, most notable for its twin octagonal towers guarding the main entrance, was until very recently a private school. Until 1722, when the line (which dated from the Norman Conquest) died out, it was home to a Lord Brereton.

Passing to the right of the church and negotiating the cattlegrid brings you onto the bridlepath – a well-trodden track giving access to the farm workers' cottages that line it. Follow the track, being sure to close the gates that you pass through, until you reach the world of tarmac again. Here, turn left and within 400 yards, on your right, is the main access to Brereton Heath Country Park. What was once a sand quarry is now a scenic lake with acres of woodland and well marked walks set alongside. This 'natural' beauty is well complemented by modern visitor facilities.

Section b-a

Pulling back onto the road and continuing in the same direction, you soon reach the A54 which you should cross and then head off down the lane to the left of the intriguingly shaped lodge. Having made your way past the sleeping policemen, a plethora of signs and a gate, you find yourself on a bridlepath crossing the land of Davenport Hall Farm. Keeping right, you quickly descend into the beautiful Dane Valley with the radio telescope at Jodrell Bank prominent on the horizon. Follow the path through all its gates and meanderings, and you'll soon find yourself ascending a series of river terraces.

This brings you to the village of Swettenham, and firstly its church. Although not as immediately striking as the more notable churches on the route, St Peter's does have an interesting history of its own. It was formerly a black and white half-timbered affair but in 1720 was encased in brick – evidence of this can be seen if you pass the church and look back.

Behind the church and a vast patrons' car park lies the Swettenham Arms. This building was initially a nunnery associated with the church but has since changed out of all recognition – whether this is a change for the better is a matter of opinion, although one view is by far the more widely held! Swettenham is a sizeable cul-de-sac and you must now follow this road round to the right, along the valley of Midge Brook. As you follow this road, an interesting diversion presents itself: take the left fork – a narrow lane forebodingly signposted "DEEP FORD – Unsuitable for cars". A steep descent brings you to the rural idyll of a cottage by a ford, although the brook is perhaps best crossed using the helpfully placed footbridge. It is then a steep climb out of the valley to rejoin the main route.

Taking the right fork, however, keeps you high above all this, albeit with a pleasing view of it. Follow the lane until you reach a T-junction where you should almost U-turn and cycle down past Swettenham Mill. The valley at the rear of the mill has been planted, over many years, with thousands of daffodil bulbs producing a stunning Spring sight and earning it the name "Daffodil Dell". (You can visit the Dell in springtime – check opening times before setting out). Make your way up the hill to meet the diversionary route and then take the first right. Follow what ·becomes Messuage Lane past a number of turn-offs and farms and over a crossroads until you are presented with a choice of turning left into Marton Hall Lane or right onto Mill Lane. Turn left but you'll later be retracing your route to this point and then cycling along Mill Lane to Newsbank.

Having first turned on to Marton Hall Lane, you'll soon have to fork left off it and will eventually reach the A34 as it passes through Marton. Turn right and head for the pleasant pub and, certainly as importantly, Marton Parish Church. St James and St Paul's proudly claims to be the oldest half-timbered church in Europe still in use, dating as it does from the fourteenth century. As striking as the exterior is, the interior is considerably more interesting with its timber skeleton clearly on view, together with fourteenth century wall-paintings and an Elizabethan parish chest amongst its treasures.

Returning to the saddle, retrace your route as far as the junction of the three lanes and continue on along Mill Lane past the mill itself until you reach the hamlet of Newsbank where you should turn left. The lane you now find yourself on should take you through Hulme Walfield and up into Congleton's Lower(!) Heath until you reach the busy A34 again. Brave the traffic in order to turn right and head down the hill towards the traffic lights at which you should turn left. This swiftly brings you to two roundabouts (separated by traffic lights) which you should head straight across, unless you wish to investigate Congleton's centre in which case you should turn off right at the second of these. Beyond the second roundabout follow the signposts up the hill to return you to the railway station you left a few, hopefully enjoyable, hours ago.

18. Crewe to Betley

Distance: 17 Miles/27km.

Route: Crewe – Shavington – Wybunbury – Wrinehill – Betley – Balterley – Barthomley – Crewe Green – Crewe.

Surface: Tarmac.

Start: Crewe Railway Station (SJ711548).

Map: O.S. 118 (the Potteries).

The Route

Set in Cheshire's "Deep South" this amiable route leaves Crewe and the Cheshire Plain to flirt with the rolling hills of Staffordshire. In doing so it takes in what is perhaps the county's most beautiful village, Barthomley; a church battling vainly against nature's attempt to reclaim the land on which it was built and mile after mile of beautiful countryside.

There is little in the way of hard climbs but some of the more narrow lanes should be travelled with caution and the ride in its entirety should take perhaps a couple of hours in the saddle.

The Journey

Section a-b

Taking as our starting point Crewe Railway Station, whose car park is actually some two hundred yards down the road next to the Royal Hotel, head first along the A534 towards Nantwich. Reaching a set of traffic lights, turn left to make your way towards Shavington. In doing so you'll pass Crewe Alexandra's Gresty Road stadium and what actually represents only a fraction of Crewe's railway-associated industry.

Passing through Shavington and across the A500(T) and then through an almost surreal landscape of poplar-lined avenues, you will find yourself in Wybunbury – most notable for its church, or at least its remnants. All that now survives of St Chad's is the fifteenth century tower: the rest of the building had to be demolished in 1978 as a result of sand movement on the hillside undermining the structure. Even then the battle against erosion was not won, with the tower listing for several years – Cheshire's answer to the leaning tower of Pisa.

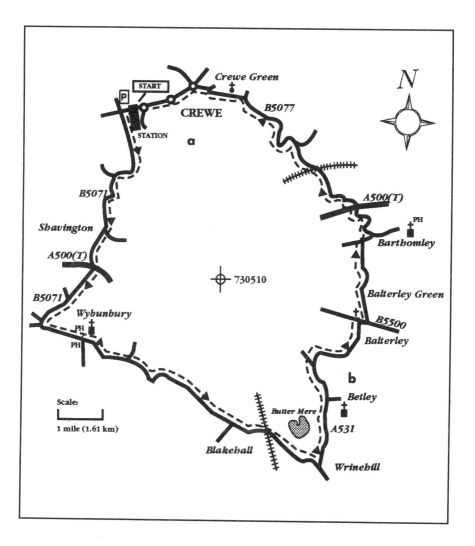

Having already passed the Swan Inn, travel a little further down the hill in order to turn left opposite the Red Lion. Following this quiet lane for the four miles to Wrinehill you'll pass the striking Lea Hall and cross over the West Coast line to find yourself, as you pass the signal box, on a brief foray into rural Staffordshire. As you descend towards Wrinehill you're presented with a view out to your left across Betley Mere and, in the far distance, perched on its hilly vantage point, Mow Cop castle folly with the south east corner of Cheshire stretched out in its entirety in between.

Turning sharply left upon reaching the main road, follow the A531 past Wrinehill's and Betley's pubs, quaint black and white cottages and some equally captivating, almost military architecture and an antiques gallery until you find yourself leaving Betley. Passing the imposing, though somewhat shabby, half-timbered hall on your left and descending the hill towards a second mere, turn right to head for Balterley immediately after what could be the definitive black and white Cheshire cottage were it not for the fact that its in Staffordshire.

This twisting narrow lane eventually brings you out onto the B5500. Here, you turn right to head for Audley and then immediately turn left onto a still narrower lane to drop down through Balterley Green until a sign welcomes you to Crewe & Nantwich Borough, "the home of the best car in the world", and therefore Cheshire.

Section b-a

Turn right at the T-junction to head for Barthomley whose church is clearly visible from some distance. You soon arrive in the heart of what many consider to be the most beautiful village in the county. Its chocolate box aesthetic – all Jacobean cottages and pretty gardens – stops short, however, of being cloying and it remains a wonder that this rural idyll exists despite its proximity, to the M6.

The black and white thatched inn – the White Lion – stands opposite the red sandstone of St Bertoline's, a church with an unsavoury claim to fame. During the Civil War some of the villagers fired upon a Royalist raiding party and then sought refuge in the church tower only to be smoked out and have twelve of their number massacred. See if you can spot the gravestones with skull-and-crossbones – might there be a connection?

The White Lion, Barthomley (Chris Rushton, Evening Sentinel)

Leaving Barthomley behind, retrace your route a third of a mile to turn right by the phone box. Crossing the bridge over Crewe's motorway link bear left until you find yourself on the B5077 which you follow through all its twists and turns until Crewe Green is reached. Here you turn left and then follow the almost gratuitous amount of signs that direct you back to Crewe Railway Station, where you began your journey.

19. Crewe, Barthomley & Wybunbury

Distance: 16 miles/26km.

Route: Crewe – Barthomley – Balterley Green – Balterley – Buddileigh – Wynbunbury – Shavington – Crewe

Surface: Tarmac, Gravel & Concrete.

Start: Crewe Railway Station (SJ712548).

Map: O.S. 118 (the Potteries).

Notes: As the A500 is a new road it is not yet marked on present 1986 1:50,000 OS Landranger maps.

The Route

The ride begins in the industrial sector of Crewe, but it continues along the A5020 into a wooded area with Crewe Hall on the left hand side of the road. Leaving the A5020 and subsequently the B5077 the route follows quiet country lanes with rolling fields and hedgerows so characteristic to the area of the Cheshire Plain.

Continuing south the ride passes through part of Staffordshire before heading west towards Wynbunbury and eventually north back to Crewe, a town well-known not only for its trains but for the production of one of the world's finest cars, the Rolls-Royce.

There are various shops, pubs, supermarkets and restaurants in Crewe. Also the Red Lion on the B5071, the Swan Inn at Wynbunbury and the Cheshire Cheese just outside Crewe.

The Journey

Section a-b

From the entrance of Crewe Station, turn right onto the A534 Nantwich road. Follow the road over the zebra crossing and drop down towards the roundabout. Make sure to get in the inside lane as the fourth exit is

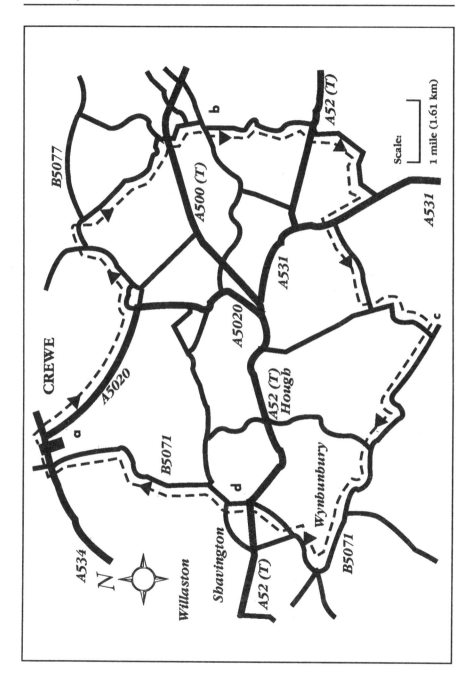

the route you will need to take.

Follow the signs for Stoke on the A5020, along the road through Crewe's industrial estate. Two miles outside Crewe, note Crewe Hall on the left. Follow the A5020 ahead to a second roundabout. Take the first exit, following signs for Alsager, five miles away at this point. A few hundred metres after the roundabout ride down the hill, between woods on the left and right owned by the Duchy of Lancaster.

Carry on along the road, up the hill to a junction where you turn right (off Old Park Road) onto the B5077 towards Alsager. Follow the road ahead and onwards around the bend, dropping down the hill as you go. At the bottom of the hill take the first road on your right. This is Barthomley Road (Barthomley village is two miles away).

Bear right at all times, and follow the signs for Barthomley, half a mile from Smiths Green. Ride over the A500(T) down the hill past Smithy Lane on the left and around the bend. Follow the road ahead until a junction marked with a red phone box, at the edge of Barthomley.

Section b-c

At the junction with the telephone box turn right, following signs for Weston and Betley. Follow the road ahead for a few hundred metres until you reach the first turning on the left. Turn left here towards Balterley and follow Deans Lane as it winds its way south.

Cross over Englesea Brook and into a wooded area. Ride up the other side of the hill through Balterley Green and across the border into Staffordshire. At the end of Deans Lane, give way at the junction before turning right onto the A52(T), following signs for Balterley Heath.

Follow the road ahead for a short distance until you reach the first road on the left, opposite a chapel on the right-hand side. Turn left here and ride along the lane as it drops down-hill through attractive farming land.

At the end of the lane, turn right onto the A531. Ride past Doddlespool Hall on the left, and do not deviate from the A531 until you reach another lane to the left. Follow this somewhat muddy and pot-holed route back into Cheshire.

A few hundred metres downhill along the lane you meet a fork in the lane at West Heath, with a house in the middle of the fork. Bear left here and continue down the hill. Ride past Anchorage Farm on the left, continuing along the bumpy lane, over a brook and up the hill.

At the top of the hill, you can see the railway line. Drop down the hill and, where the lane curves sharply to the right, turn onto a gravel track.

Follow the track then go over the railway towards Gonsley Green Farm. Bear left through the farm yard onto a concrete lane and follow it ahead to a junction.

Section c-d

At the junction, turn right. Follow the road ahead as it winds its way between hedgerows and, eventually, turn into Wrine Hill Road approximately half a mile outside Wynbunbury. This road is part of the Cheshire Cycleway.

In the village of Wynbunbury, turn right onto the B5071 (Bridge Street). Ride up the hill with Wynbunbury Church on the right and the Red Lion pub on the left. Follow the bend around to the left with the Swan Inn on the right. Follow the B5071 out of Wynbunbury, onwards towards Shavington and stop at the junction with the A52.

Section d-a

Cross the A52 and follow signs for Crewe on the B5071. Follow the road ahead through Shavington.

Approximately a mile from the centre of Crewe, a bend bears right with the Cheshire Cheese pub on the right.

Follow the B5071, watching for signs for the railway station. At the junction with the A534 Nantwich road, turn right by the traffic lights and continue along the road to the station.

20. Crewe, Shavington & Blakelow

Distance: 10.5 miles/16.5km.

Route: Crewe Station – Shavington – Hough – Dove House Farm – Wybunbury – Haymoor Green – Blakelow – Willaston – Crewe Station.

Surface: Tarmac.

Start: Crewe Railway Station (SJ712548); Car parks are well sign-posted just off the A534 past the station. Alternatively there are many side streets suitable for parking in the vicinity of the station.

Map: O.S. 118 (the Potteries).

The Route

This starts and finishes at Crewe Railway Station. It is one of the largest and busiest railway junctions in the country, bringing together lines from Scotland, Manchester, North and South Wales, The South and Derby. The town itself grew around the railway during the industrial revolution and depends on the railway for much of the employment in the area.

The route goes out by the some of the railway buildings into the South Cheshire countryside. A quiet B Road is followed out to Shavington then along peaceful country lanes through Hough, joining the Cheshire Cycleway just before the picturesque village of Wybunbury. The route then comes back to the station through Willaston joining the main A534.

A number of pubs are situated along the ride providing suitable refreshment when required.

The Journey

Section a-b

Starting from the station concourse, turn left along the A534 towards Nantwich. After 300 yards turn left into Gresty Road, the first road on your left. Crewe Alexandra Football Club is on your left as you come to

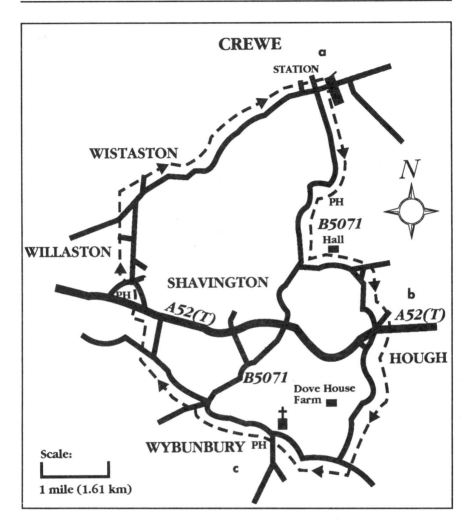

a junction. Bear left here (almost carrying on in a straight line) along the B5071 towards Shavington. Go down the slight hill and under the railway bridge, after which the road bends round to the right. Another right hand bend is followed by a sharp left bend with the Cheshire Cheese Public House on your left.

Continue along this road for about $^3/_4$ mile. 300 yards after entering Shavington there is a sharp right-hand bend with a turning on the left.

Turn left here into Weston Lane. After a few hundred yards the road goes down a slight hill and past the Hall on your left. 400 yards further on turn right by the post box into Back Lane. After half a mile, turn right at the mini-crossroads and 20 yards further on you will come to the busy A52(T).

Section b-c

Go straight ahead at the crossroads along Cobbs Lane, with a petrol station on your left. Continue along this lane through the small hamlet of Hough. Just out of Hough the hedge on the right of the lane disappears, revealing a lovely view of Wybunbury Church. On a clear day, the Welsh mountains can be seen in the far distance.

Go past Dove House Farm and down a slight hill to a T-junction at the bottom. Opposite the junction is sign indicating the Cheshire Cycleway. Turn right here and carry on towards Wybunbury. Three-quarters of a mile further on, you come to the junction meeting the B5071. Wybunbury Church is on your right and the Red Lion Public House is opposite. Turn right here up the hill with the Swan Inn at the top. Continue on through Wybunbury, past the rather more modern St Chads Church. At the right hand bend just coming out of Wybunbury turn right down Wybunbury Lane following the sign indicating Nantwich.

Section c-a

Continue towards Haymoor Green and after a little under a mile, turn right and carry on until you reach the busy A52(T) again. Turn left at the junction and then 300 yards further on, turn right into Wybunbury Road, the Horseshoe pub being on your left (sign to Willaston).

After about 400 yards the road straightens and enters Willaston. Continue along here, over the level crossing to the junction with the busy A534. Turn right here onto the A534 and follow the road back to Crewe Station.

21. Crewe and Church Minshull

Distance: 16 miles/26km.

Route: Crewe – Coppenhall Moss – Warmingham – Occlestone Green – Walley's Green – Church Minshull – Bradfield Green – Barrow's Green – Crewe.

Surface: Tarmac.

Start: Crewe Railway Station (SJ711548).

Map: O.S. 118 (the Potteries).

The Route

Taking in the endearingly gentle undulations of the Cheshire Plain this easy route throws into almost stark contrast the county's rural heritage and the Latter-day incursions of the nineteenth and twentieth century world.

The ride starts and finishes in Crewe – one of the more famous by-products of the Industrial Revolution, a mere two hundred years ago. Appearances, however, can be deceptive – Crewe, along with its more obviously ancient neighbour Nantwich, appears in the Domesday Survey of 1086!

To be fair, Crewe would never have grown to the size it has had the decision not been taken in the 1830's to shift the rail engineering works from Edge Hill in Liverpool to a site not far from Nantwich. Our route moves away from this urban upstart to lose itself amongst the dairy farms and picture postcard villages of central Cheshire, and passes any number of welcoming hostelries.

The ride should only take a couple of hours and is generally untaxing although, should you attempt this with younger cyclists in tow, care would need to be taken in negotiating Crewe itself.

The Journey

Section a-b

Although those arriving by car will find parking spaces considerably more plentiful in the vicinity of the "Railway Age" (some three-quarters of a mile into the ride), we'll take as our starting point Crewe Railway Station. Turning left onto the A534 towards Nantwich, you'll soon (within a few hundred yards) need to turn right at the first set of traffic lights to head for the town centre. Rolling down the hill and under the Chester line you will find yourself at the first of three roundabouts where you should turn right, go straight across and straight across again respectively. However, in doing this two interesting detours present themselves. At the second roundabout, a right turn will bring you to the "Railway Age" – a tourist/train-buff orientated attraction which has an appeal stretching beyond the anorak brigade and is well worth a visit.

Continuing on, a left turn at the second roundabout would soon bring you to Crewe's tourist information office, should you wish to investigate the town, and then the town centre which, to be honest, has little appeal unless you have an unbridled passion for retail chains and shopping malls. Returning to the route however, after crossing the third roundabout you should turn right at the second set of traffic lights – that is, those that present the first opportunity to pass under the railway line. Follow this road until you reach a T-junction, where you should turn left and within a couple of hundred yards you'll reach a roundabout over-looked by The Cross Keys pub. A right turn will swiftly bring you out into the fresh air of the Cheshire countryside, and in the distance Congleton Edge in the east and the Peckforton Hills in the west begin to come into view.

Section b-c

Having passed the house with the twisted brick pillars, you'll reach a T-junction at which you should turn left and then right. Following this road for a couple of miles brings you to Warmingham – a pleasant hamlet clustered around a bridge over the River Wheelock, which the "Bear's Paw" overlooks. Continuing up out of Warmingham there is, tucked away on the left, a tiny craft centre worthy of investigation if such places are to your taste.

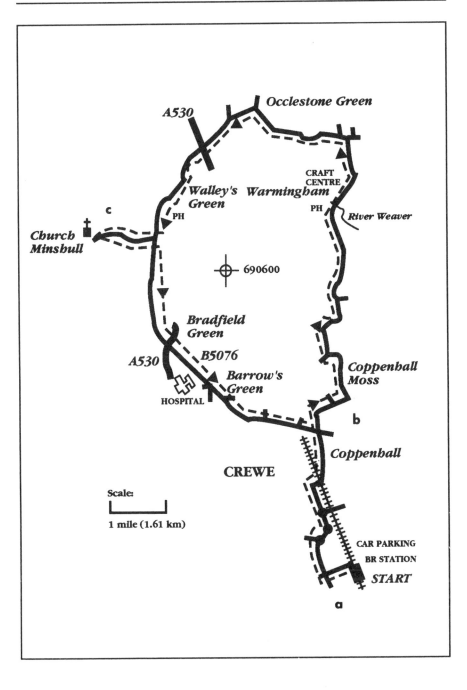

Following the road on you'll eventually be forced to turn left and to cycle past, as you re-cross the River Wheelock, the quaint black and white Mill Lodge almost completely shrouded by conifers. Following the road through another dip and bearing left through Occlestone Green you'll soon emerge onto A530 which you should follow back towards Crewe. As you cross the bridge over the railway the elegant Wimboldsley Hall comes into view and shortly after, standing closer to the road, the similarly styled "Vernin Inn".

As you reach Walley's Green you should fork right past the Celtic cross that commemorates Queen Victoria's diamond jubilee. A right turn brings you swiftly to the Shropshire Union canal and then you'll drop down the hill to the River Weaver and Church Minshull – a gorgeous picture postcard village with a fine opportunity to break your journey in the shape of a real ale pub. For those, however, disinclined to seek the refreshment that "The Badger" has to offer there is a Post Office and shop tucked away behind it. Amongst the black and white cottages, look out in particular for the precarious room above the porch of the cottage opposite the church.

Section c-a

Retracing your route back up the hill, follow the lane round to the right past what is now the U.R.C. chapel to rejoin the A530 momentarily at Bradfield Green – a place with little.to commend it save perhaps the "Coach and Horses".

A right and, almost immediately, a left turn leaves you heading back into Crewe along the B5076, passing on your right an example of early 1970s "architecture". Such are the delights of Leighton Hospital. A left turn at the roundabout that is quickly reached brings you back to the roundabout overlooked by "The Cross Keys" from which you should be able to retrace your steps to bring to an end this untesting but pleasant cycle route.

22. Crewe, Moston and Willaston

Distance: 26 miles.

Route: Crewe Railway Station – Englesea House – Haslington – Moston green – Warmingham – Coppenhall Moss – Church Minshull – Worleston – Willaston – Crewe Railway Station.

Surface: Tarmac.

Start: Crewe Railway Station (SJ711548).

Map: O.S. 118 (the Potteries).

The Route

This route is for those cyclists who are after a bit of distance under their wheels. Though the ride is not too taxing as far as hills are concerned, the 26 miles are ample compensation. For those who wish to finish the ride mid-way through, the route cuts across main roads which lead back to the centre of Crewe. Initially the ride follows the quickest route into the countryside via the A5020, but soon travels along quiet country lanes. There are numerous pubs and cafes in Crewe and along the journey.

The Journey

Section a-b

Leave Crewe station and turn right onto the A534 Nantwich road. Follow this busy 'A' road over the zebra crossing and go downhill to the roundabout. Take the fourth exit off the roundabout onto the A5020 towards Stoke. Continue along the road past Crewe's industrial estate and Crewe Hall, then follow the A5020 along until reaching the roundabout. Take the first exit and follow the sign for Alsager which is five miles away. Follow the road downhill, through woods owned by the Duchy of Lancaster.

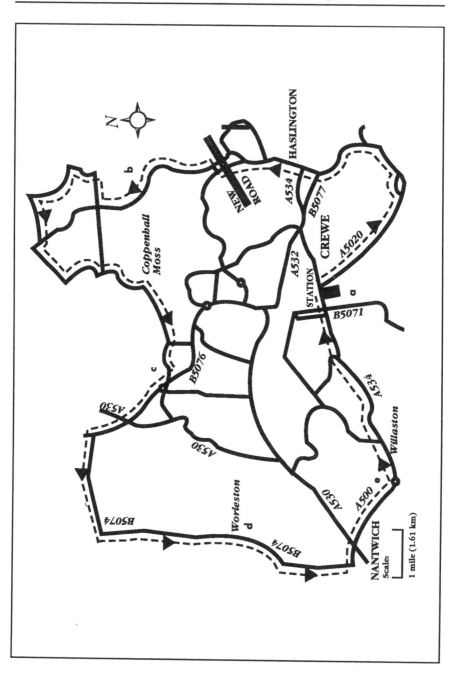

Ride along the road and up to the top of the hill to a junction at the corner of a bend. Turn left here onto the B5077. A third of a mile down the road, the road curves to the left and drops down a gentle hill. At a sharp left-hand bend at the bottom of the hill, ride straight ahead off the B5077 and onwards up the lane towards Haslington, half a mile away.

Ride a short distance along the lane until it meets the A534. Turn right and ride through the centre of Haslington until the A534 bends to the right. At this point, turn left into 'The Dingle'. On the corner is a telephone box and just after the corner is a chapel on the left.

Continue through the residential area of Haslington over Fowle Brook and into the open countryside. Ride over the dual carriageway and take the first turning right towards Elton and Warmingham. After turning into the lane, ride a few hundred yards to a second junction. Turn left onto Clay Lane, follow the road ahead and ride under the pylons. Approximately a mile down Clay Lane, follow a sharp bend left. Ride into the Moston along Clay Lane until reaching a large railway tunnel.

Section b-c

Ride under the railway line and follow the wide lane ahead as it curves to the right. There will be large ponds ('flashes' locally) to the left and right of the road. Continue to a junction, turn right at the junction onto Hall Lane and follow the route ahead.

Ride towards Ettiley Heath and take the first left down Red Lane just after a large warehouse. The large area of water is Watch Lane Flash, on the left of Red Lane. The lane curves left and right until it meets a bend to the right. At this point Red Lane becomes Watch Lane. (Make sure not to follow the dead-end alongside Watch Lane Flash). This lane curves right and then sharply left around a blind bend before meeting a junction. Here, turn left with a telephone box on the left-hand side. Follow Plant Lane ahead and pass through Moston Green.

After Moston Green, take the first left down Green Lane. Pass Moston Flash on the right and ride straight ahead to another junction. Turn right onto an unmarked lane. Follow the road to a junction on a bend. Turn left here onto School Lane and ride towards Warmingham. Drop down past a craft centre on the right and over the river Wheelock, passing a church on the left. Follow what is now the Warmingham road ahead and ride out of Warmingham. After a mile, ride under the pylons and take a right-hand bend into Coppenhall Moss.

The Warmingham road continues as Parker's Road. Go over the railway line and drop down into the outer suburbs of Crewe. At the end of Parker's Lane turn right onto the B5076. Ride ahead to a roundabout.

Section c-d

At the roundabout, take the third exit along the B5076. Ride under the pylons and follow the road ahead. At the end of the B5076, turn right at the junction onto the A530. Take the first left towards Church Minshull, three miles away. A mile or so up the road, follow a sharp bend left, following signs for Church Minshull. Follow the road ahead over the Shropshire Union canal and the River Weaver.

At the junction, turn left onto the B5074 and follow the road ahead out of Church Minshull. (Note the next five miles of the route follows the B5074 as there are few country lanes leading back to Crewe). You soon ride over the Shropshire Union Canal and, another mile along the road, ride over the railway line. Follow the road ahead into Warleston shortly after passing over the railway line.

Section d-e

Follow the B5074 out of Warleston under some pylons and past Rookery Hall Hotel on the left. A mile and a half down the road, pass the Cheshire College of Agriculture on the right. Shortly afterwards you will meet the junction of the A51(T).

Turn left following signs for the A500. Upon reaching the roundabout take the first exit following signs for Crewe railway station which is now four miles away.

Section e-a

Ride over the river Weaver and under a set of pylons continuing to follow signs for the A500. After about a mile and a half, arrive at a second roundabout. Once again take the first exit onto the A534 into Willaston.

From Willaston, Crewe station is three miles away. From here on the route will follow the A534 through Crewe's residential suburbs before entering into the town centre and finally arriving at the entrance of Crewe railway station.

23. Cuddington and Delamere

Distance: 15 miles.

Route: Cuddington – Acton Bridge – River Weaver – Hatch Mere – Delamere Forest – Oakmere – Cuddington.

Surface: Tarmac, with some bridleways which can become muddy.

Start: Cuddington Railway Station (SJ602716)

Map: O.S. 117 (Chester) and O.S. 118 (the Potteries).

The Route

The route is generally easy but there are a couple of steepish climbs (and descents) on the Sandstone ridge. The early part of the route follows the River Weaver which has been dredged and by-passed in places by the weaver Navigation and eventually joins the Mersey estuary just beyond Frodsham. The Weaver Navigation was originally used as a means of carrying salt from the Cheshire salt mines.

The route also passes through Delamere Forest, and some of the tracks through the forest have recently been designated as cycle routes. The remainder of the ride is mainly on typically narrow and twisty Cheshire country lanes.

The Journey

Section a-b

From Cuddington railway station cross the main A49 at the traffic lights along Norley Road, then turn almost immediately right down Mill Lane. At the end of Mill Lane turn left and first right after about 50 yards. Follow this lane for half a mile and turn left at the T-junction and then next right on Onston Lane through Onston. At the next T-junction, turn right on Station Road.This is the B5153 and, after half a mile, it enters Acton Bridge.

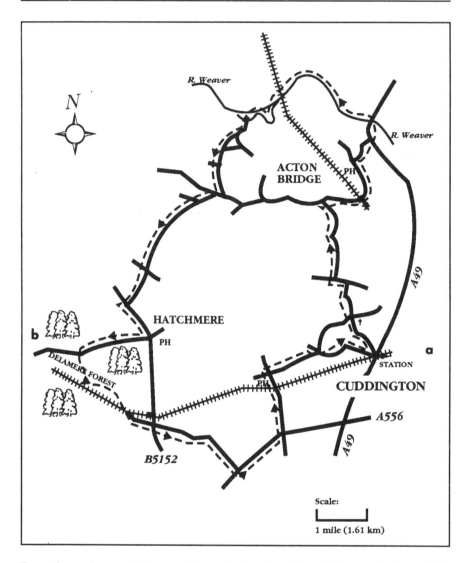

Pass the railway station and turn left at the Hazel Pear pub along Hill Top Lane. The road eventually bends to the right into Acton Lane and goes steeply down-hill. At the foot of the hill, it joins the A49 where you turn left and cross the swing bridge over the River Weaver. As the road is narrow over the bridge, it is safer to walk along the footpath at this point. The swing bridge carrying the A49 was built over 60 years ago and is still operational. There are two pubs just past the bridge, the Leigh Arms and the Horn Inn.

Turn left immediately after the bridge on the track along the edge of the river, parts of which have been dredged and by-passed by the Weaver Navigation. After about a mile, cross the river and then go over the locks by the footbridge. Turn right along the path underneath the Dutton viaduct which carries the main London to Liverpool and London to Glasgow railway lines.

After about half a mile, at Pickering's Wharf the path turns left into a country lane. Stay on this as it climbs uphill ignoring turns to left and right. At the T-junction at the end, turn right then left after 200 yards down a narrow lane. Take the left fork after 300 yards and climb up the Sandstone ridge.

Go straight over the next cross-roads and turn left at the T-junction on the B5152, soon passing Hatch Mere and the Carriers Inn. At the Forest Gate Cafe, turn right into Delamere Forest along Ashton Road.

Section b-a

Follow the road through the forest, passing the Barnsbridge Gate car park after about half a mile. Continue for a further half mile to a track on the left signed to Acton Bridge, Delamere and Kelsall. Turn left here and stay on the main track, following the 'cycle path' route marks in the direction of Delamere Station. There are some good places to stop in the forest for picnics; note that bicycles are not allowed except on the designated paths.

After two miles, the track crosses the railway line and turns left along a road. Delamere railway station, which is at the end of the road, is a good place to stop for refreshments. Cross the road at the station towards Delamere Forest Golf Club. Pass the clubhouse on your left and, at the fork, head right. This eventually comes out on the A556, where you turn left. This is a busy road and it may be safer to use the path to your left.

After a mile, turn left (signed to Norley) at the cross-roads. At the top of the hill, turn right on Cuddington Lane. A road joins from the left but you should keep straight on to the cross-roads on the A49; Cuddington station is straight ahead.

24. Disley into Derbyshire

Distance: 20 miles/32km

Route: Disley – High Lane – Middlewood Way – Middlewood Station – Higher Poynton – Pott Shrigley – Kettleshulme – Whaley Bridge – Chinley – New Mills – Disley.

Surface: Tarmac & sandy gravel.

Start: Disley Railway Station (SJ 996854).

Map: O.S. 118 (the Potteries) and O.S. 110 (Sheffield) and O.S. 119 (Buxton) and O.S. Landranger 109 (Manchester and surrounding area).

The Route

The route out of Disley heads past Lyme Country Park. From here it travels downhill on the A6 for a short distance and joins the

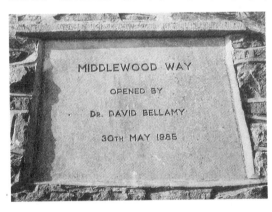

Middlewood Way just past High Lane. This disused railway line was reopened as a recreational route by David Bellamy in 1985.

From Higher Poynton the route winds its way to Pott Shrigley, climbs steadily into the Peak National Park and heads towards the Derbyshire border. From Whaley Bridge, we ride alongside the River Goyt, north west towards New Mills and returns to Disley Station via the A6.

There are almost too many pubs to choose from: the Rams Head, Disley; the Red Lion, High Lane; Boar's Head, Higher Poynton; the Bulls Head and The Swan, Kettleshulme; the White Horse, Whaley Bridge; the Squirrels Pub in Chinley and there's even a Little Chef on the A6.

The Journey

Section a-b

From Disley Station, turn left onto the A6. The road climbs a gentle gradient and winds its way past Lyme Country Park with its historical house and grounds. A few hundred yards after the entrance to Lyme Park, you enter the Stockport suburb of High Lane.

On leaving High Lane, note the pylons which cross the road. These pylons run parallel to the Middlewood Way. Just before the pylons there is a bridge and, at this point, Middlewood Way is signposted.

After negotiating the style and the steps, head south along this disused railway cutting. **Note:** Middlewood Way is also used by horses and pedestrians, so care should be taken when cycling along this route.

Ride along the Middlewood Way, past Middlewood Station and under the bridges towards Higher Poynton, where there is an excellent picnic site based on the old station platform; there's also a convenient café and the Boar's Head pub. Lock up your bike and go through the stile above the platform to pay a visit. To ignore these delights, ride up the ramp at the north end of the platform, go through the kissing gate and turn right on Shrigley Road North.

Section b-c

Whichever way you left Higher Poynton, follow the signs for Pott Shrigley, 3 miles away. Ride over the Middlewood Way and follow the road through a narrow tunnel under the Macclesfield Canal.

The road skirts Lyme Park (passing West Park Gate) and from here there are superb views across the Cheshire Plain and, on a clear day, you can see the Frodsham Hills, the Clwydian range, Alderley Edge and Greater Manchester in one panoramic sweep.

A few hundred yards after riding past Shrigley Hall's Golf Club on the left you arrive at a junction. Turn left here and follow the signs for Pott Shrigley. The village is now only a mile away. Ride past the church on the right and take the first left (signposted to Whaley Bridge). The route climbs into the Peak District National Park with impressive views to the south. Follow the road ahead to a junction, turn left and ride down the 10% hill into Kettleshulme on the B5470.

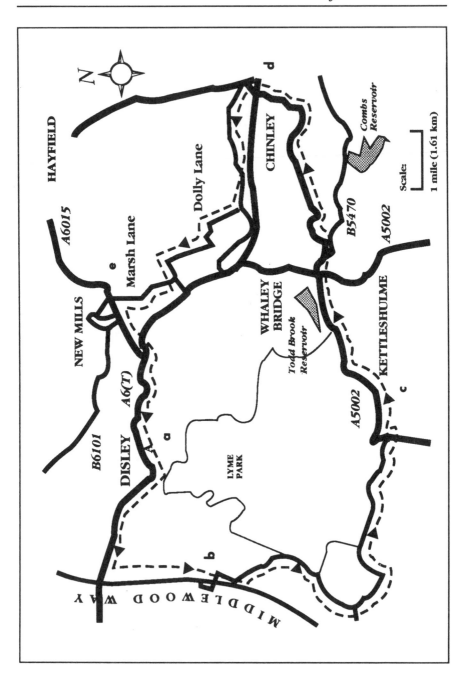

Section c-d

Ride through Kettleshulme and follow the B5470 to Whaley Bridge. On the left of the road before entering Whaley Bridge is Toddbrook Reservoir. Ride past this, across the Cheshire/Derbyshire Boundary and down the hill into Whaley Bridge.

At the traffic lights, ride straight ahead on B5470 towards Chapel-en-le-Frith until you reach the Board Inn on the left. A few hundred yards after this, take the first left up Eccles Road. Cross over the railway line and continue, with views of Nab Tor, Black Edge and Combs Reservoir. Follow the Eccles road past Eccles Pike and down the hill towards the edge of Chapel-en-le-Frith.

Section d-e

At the end of Eccles Road, turn left at the junction onto Crossing Road. Follow this to the first turning on the right. Turn right and ride down Charley Lane under the A6 and up the hill past the disused mill, towards the A624. At the end of Charley Lane, turn left onto the A624 and ride towards Chinley. The A624 joins the B6062. Follow the road ahead on the B6062 and ignore any signs for Glossop.

Continue on the B6062 out of Chinley towards Leaden Knowl and Brierley Green. After riding through Brierley Green take the first right up Dolly Lane. Follow this, past the electricity substation. Ignore turnings for Furness Vale and head towards New Mills on what is now Marsh Lane.

Section e-a

At the end of Marsh Lane turn left onto Church Road (the A6015) and ride towards the centre of New Mills. Follow the A6015 up the hill, past the confectionery factory on the right, over New Mills Station and on to the traffic lights.

At the traffic lights, turn left onto the A6 and ride towards the sign posts for Manchester and Stockport. Follow the road ahead until you cross from Derbyshire back into Cheshire. Ride for approximately a mile and a half back to Disley Station and the end of the route.

25. Disley and New Mills

Distance: 10 miles/16km.

Route: Disley Station – New Mills – New Mills Station – Low Leighton – Clough Head – Furness Vale Station – Lowe Ends – Disley Station.

Surface: Tarmac, Grass, Hardcore.

Start: Disley Railway Station (SJ996854).

Map: O.S. Landranger 109 (Manchester and surrounding area) and O.S. 119 (Buxton, Matlock and the Dove Dale area).

The Route

Fountain Square, Disley

This route is one of two rides which starts in Cheshire and includes some of the steep hillsides of Derbyshire. The route is only 10 miles, but very hilly – so you really do need a good range of gears, strong legs and good brakes. Check all of these before you start!

One of the best features is the scenery. To the east you can see the rolling hills of the Peak District, including Kinder Scout. There are also good views along the Goyt Valley towards New Mills and Disley and, looking the other way, towards Whaley Bridge and Chapel-en-le-Frith.

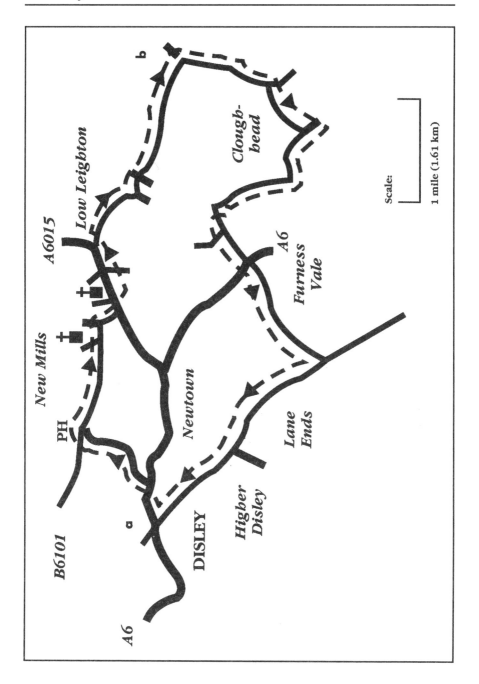

The route is mainly on tarmac roads, and there are a couple of adventurous bridleways. These are rough and can be muddy. You'll find plenty of pubs and shops along the route to maintain your energy.

The Journey

Section a-b

Leave Disley railway station and turn right, through the centre of town. Take the fourth left down Red House Lane, just before the White Lion pub. NOTE: Beware of juggernauts on this narrow lane, going to the drum factory on Red House Lane, especially on weekdays. Follow the road downhill, under a narrow railway bridge, over the Peak Forest Canal and under another railway line. At the T-junction, turn right into Waterside Road, and go round a sharp left-hand hairpin. Follow the road over the River Goyt and continue uphill to the crossroads. Turn right and follow the road (B6101) for three-quarters of a mile until you reach New Mills; go past the BR station on your right and follow the road downhill, round to the right and through the town centre.

At the bottom of the road, turn left at the traffic lights onto Church Road (A6015). Follow this road for three-quarters of a mile until you reach Low Leighton. Turn right down Laneside with the Hare and Hounds pub on the left. Follow this road up to the top until, after a mile, the road deteriorates at a crossroads into a rough track. This is on the fringe of the Peak District, and for the next a mile and a half the terrain is rocky, muddy and, more often than not, wet. But fun!

At the crossroads go straight on and you will soon reach a series of gates (make sure that you shut them behind you). After about three-quarters of a mile from the first crossroads, you reach a second crossroads; turn right here, following a wall on your right to the bottom of the track – you are now leaving the Peak District and travelling back down into the bottom of the valley.

Section b-a

Turn right at the end of the track, and after a few hundred yards, turn left. After a short downhill run through Clough Head you reach a T-junction, where you turn right. Follow the road for a mile and a half, past a water works and under a railway line. Then, turn left and continue over both the River Goyt and the Peak Forest Canal. Go over a level crossing, with The Crossings pub on your left and head up to the A6. You are now in Furness Vale.

Go straight across the A6 and up Yearsley Lane, taking your first right turn into Diglee Road. Follow the road until it starts to deteriorate and, soon, it forks. Turn left here and, at the gate to Diglee Farm, go straight through the farmyard and through another gate to a bridleway.

At the top of the bridleway, turn right onto a road. The views from this point are particularly impressive – behind you there's the Goyt Valley and the Peak District; to the right the valley which you have been cycling through, and straight on are views of Stockport.

This road leads to Higher Disley and eventually back into Disley. At the bottom of the hill, continue to the main road and turn left. This brings you back to the railway station.

26. Goostrey, Swettenham and Congleton

Distance: 23 miles/37km.

Route: Goostrey Station – Twemlow Green – Swettenham – Brereton Heath – Congleton – Somerford Booths – Swettenham Heath – Withington – Jodrell Bank – Goostrey – Goostrey Station.

Surface: Mostly tarmac, with gravel and hardcore.

Start: Goostrey Station car-park (783967). Car parking is available to non-BR users for a modest fee.

Map: O.S. 118 (the Potteries).

The Route

This route passes very close to Jodrell Bank and it's worth a quick detour to this landmark and place of scientific interest. A pleasant picnic can be had at Brereton Heath Country Park and there are pubs in Swettenham, Lower Withington, Withington and Goostrey.

The Journey

Section a-b

Cycle out of the car-park and turn left, over the railway bridge. You pass into Twemlow and what appears to be an underground reservoir on the right, before arriving at a T-junction. Go left to a second T-junction, left again onto the A535, and then first right, Forty Acre Lane, signposted "Swettenham 3". As you turn right, the Yellow Broom restaurant will be on your left. Continue cycling into Kermincham, past the entrance to Kermincham Hall on the right. Jodrell Bank's radio telescope is on the left. Turn right, signposted "Swettenham 1.5", just after Kermincham Lodge on the right-hand side.

After around 700m you arrive at a small cross roads; go right, signposted as a dead end and with partially obscured signs to Chestnut, Ash Tree and Cross Lane farms. Keep cycling past the farms on the left and right, and follow the track down and to the right.

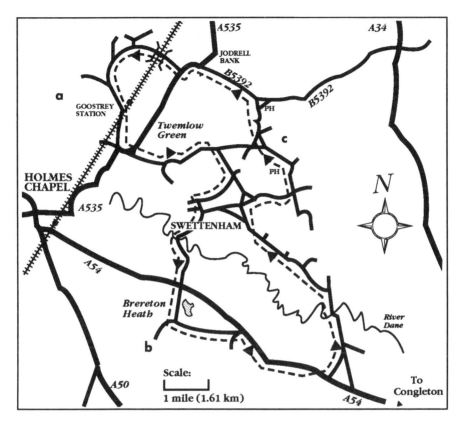

After around a kilometre from the crossroads you arrive at a newly developed farm. The track continues straight on, while another one drops sharply down to the left, through trees. Turn left and go down the gravel track, with landscaped pools further along on the left and right. Cross the brook over the bridge and up the steep concrete track on the other side.

At the top of the slope you emerge at a right angle onto a narrow concrete track with a double wooden gate opposite; go left here and follow the track to the right. You arrive at a road junction with a farm on your immediate left, an old farmhouse on the right and a phone box and bus stop further up on the right. This is Swettenham. There's a choice of left or straight on; you continue ahead, past the cottages on the left and right and past the church with its war memorial. At the rear of the church is the Swettenham Arms, a free house.

Follow the road straight on out of Swettenham, past the church as it bends to the right and downhill. The track curves to the left slightly and you pass a sign on the left indicating a bridle-path straight ahead. Across the track in front is a wooden gate, festooned with signs warning people to keep dogs on leads. Another sign says 'trespassers will be prosecuted.' The farmer is obviously very keen for you to stay off his land, so keep on the track. Progress through the side-gate on the left and continue riding as the track becomes a narrow gravel/dirt surface that could become muddy in winter.

Ride over the bridge over the River Dane and through another wooden gate with more livestock warnings and private fishing signs. Follow the track uphill as it twists and turns, swapping from hard-core to tarmac surfaces. As the track crests the hill, keep straight on towards the farm buildings directly ahead.

As you approach the buildings you will have to pass through a metal gate, beyond which is a smooth tarmac surface with verges and high hedges, the other side of which are farmhouses. Cycle over the speed bumps and up to a cross roads. Be careful, you have just joined the fast moving A54.

Take the road straight across, slightly to the right and towards the densely packed trees ahead. A few hundred metres down the road, you will be able to see Brereton Heath Park with its lake. This can be a pleasant stop for a picnic, and there may also be an ice cream van in the car park, but note the signs warning against swimming. Nothing is charged to go in but the car-park gates are closed at 8.30pm.

Section b-c

If no stop is made, keep cycling straight on along the road, with trees on your left and double yellow lines on either side. You arrive at a small crossroads with a house on the right. The road you have been following goes straight on, whilst another road goes off to the left and a small track marked as a dead end goes right. Turn left, skirting around the edge of the wood.

Cycle along this straight road, with the woods on the left and fields on the right. After just over half a kilometre you pass a white house on the right. Further up, you start to pass houses on the left and right-hand side of the road; continue cycling until you come to a T-junction with the A54. Go right and follow the A54 for around 2 kilometres. (There is a path here if necessary. The road is quite narrow and can be fast moving).

Take the first proper road on the left, just after a road on the right. The road you want (Chelford Road) is signposted 'Somerford Booths 2, Swettenham 4. Follow this past houses on the left. Around half a kilometre from the A54 junction, a road merges to the right from Congleton; carry on cycling in the same direction, signposted to Somerford Booths and Swettenham. Shortly after this, a second road merges from the right; keep straight on.

The road starts to drop downhill with a stone wall on the left and trees on either side. Cross over the River Dane before climbing up through trees on the other side.

The road forks, with the road you have been following going straight on and Swettenham road, signposted 'Swettenham 2', going off to the left; take this back towards Swettenham. Go across a small crossroads and past a cluster of semi-detached houses on the right. Just under a kilometre further down the road on the left you pass the entrance to Swettenham Hall, with lots of 'private' signs.

Ignore the road to the left, signposted 'Swettenham village only' and cycle straight on, dropping down the hill and up the other side. Take the first road on the right, just at the top of the hill. As you cycle along, a road will merge from the left with a farm track directly opposite; continue straight on until you reach a cross roads where you must give way. Go left here and follow the road up to the Black Swan pub on the left (a free house).

Section c-a

Continue cycling in the same direction. Just around the corner, a sign proclaims 'Borough of Macclesfield – Lower Withington'.

Pass through Lower Withington, shortly after which a tree-lined road merges from the left, whilst straight ahead Jodrell Bank's main radio telescope can be seen. Follow the road straight on until you reach a T-junction where. Go right, signposted to Chelford and Macclesfield. Follow this until you reach the Red Lion pub on the right hand side of the road where you go left, signposted to Chelford.

Cycle along this up to another T-junction, this time with the B5392. This is Withington. Go left and, as you cycle away from the village, you see Lower Withington Parish Hall to the left and a road off to the right to Chelford. Cycle straight on all the way up to a T-junction with the A535.

Go left, signposted 'Holmes Chapel', past the University of Manchester Department of Botany on the right, following the road as it turns round to the left and drops downhill. You want the road at the bottom on the right, before the main road climbs back up on the other side.

Once onto this road, keep going, past the track on the left and the woods on the right and up the incline. Pass under the railway bridge and continue cycling as a road fringed with pine trees merges from the right. Carry straight on, past the houses on the left up to the junction. Turn left and keep straight on as a road joins from the right. After a short distance, you'll see the church at Goostrey ahead of you. Drop downhill and up again with houses on the left and right, up to a T-junction, with St. Luke's church on your immediate left. Go left past the Red Lion on your left, up the slight incline and just out of Goostrey to the station on your left.

A traditional Cheshire cottage in Twemlow

27. Holmes Chapel, Brereton Green and Twemlow Green

Distance: 13 miles/21km.

Route: Holmes Chapel Railway Station – Brereton Green – Brereton Heath – Twemlow Green – Holmes Chapel Railway Station.

Surface: Tarmac, mud and gravel.

Start: Holmes Chapel Railway Station (SJ767670)

Map: O.S. 118 (the Potteries).

The Route

This route uses minor roads and bridleways in and around the outskirts of Holmes Chapel, and stays away from busy main roads, apart from about a mile around Holmes Chapel. There are three off-road sections, two being "RUPPs" (roads used as public paths) and one a bridleway.

Brereton Hall (an attractive old hall, now a school) is on the route and Jodrell Bank Radio Telescope is prominent. The journey should take the average cyclist around 2 hours. Mostly flat cycling, with just a few inclines to build up a thirst.

The Journey

Section a-b

Leave Holmes Chapel Railway Station and turn right. Follow the road up to a crossroads and go straight ahead onto the B5308 (Chester road). At the end of this road turn left onto the A54 and cycle until you reach Broad Lane on your left. Turn here and continue over the motorway and up to a T-junction. Take a left here and you'll soon go over the M6 in the opposite direction. Stay on this road for about a mile and a half until you reach the T-junction at Brereton Green.

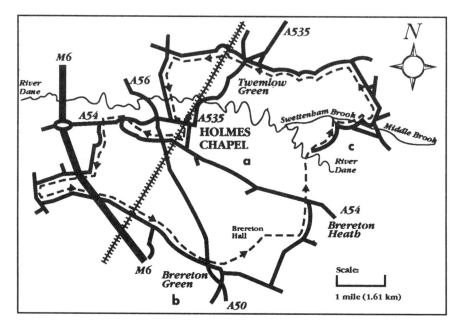

Section b-c

Turn right onto Newcastle Road North and then take an immediate left onto Newcastle Road South. At the next left turning, go left and follow the road through an archway, up to a fork in the road. Cycle down the road which goes off to the right and continue past Brereton Hall, then up to a track on the right. Turn onto this, go through a gate and you will soon arrive at a small crossroads.

Go left here and follow the road up to another small crossroads. Continue straight ahead, through a gate and onto a track which leads off to the right. Stay on this track (open and *close* the gates you encounter) cycling past the Swettenham Arms Pub and the church on your left. Now follow the road round to the right and then turn left, heading down towards the ford. Once you have crossed the ford, turn left at the T-junction and follow the road straight down to the next T-junction. Turn left here and then turn right onto Twemlow Road where the main road goes round to the left.

Section c-a

Go down Twemlow Road and continue, over a railway bridge and up to a small crossroads. Turn left here onto a narrow road, following it to the right and then left onto a track (RUPP) before Hollins Farm. Cycle downhill to a bridge over a river, and then uphill to a housing area. Stay on the road ahead of you until you reach the A535. Turn left and then turn right after the railway bridge onto Manor Lane. Continue up to the A54 (Station Road) and turn right. You soon arrive back at the start point on your right.

The impressive railway viaduct, Homes Chapel

28. Knutsford: Tatton & Mobberley

Distance: 17.2 miles/27.5km.

Route: Knutsford – Tatton Park – Rostherne – Ashley – Mobberley – Ollerton – Plumley – Tatton – Knutsford

Surface: Tarmac.

Start: Knutsford Station or King Street Car Park (SJ763784). King Street is Knutsford's (one way) High Street.

Map: O.S. 118 (the Potteries).

The Route: This ride passes through Tatton Park with its parkland, gardens, mansion, farm, old hall, restaurant, shop, deer park and boating lake. Many special events are held at the park such as Classic Car Shows, Concerts, and Craft Fairs. You will need to sort any 'extra curricula' activities yourselves as a thorough explanation would be complicated and may be subject to change. A leaflet is available at the entrance to Tatton Park, with a map and costs of admission (although cyclists enter free). This can be obtained from payment booths on entrance to the estate.

NOTE: This route makes use of roads in Tatton Park, which is open almost every day of the year; in the unlikely event of the park being closed, refer to O.S. Landranger 118 to work out a simple detour.

There are numerous food and drink outlets in Knutsford, plus The Church Inn, Mobberley, the Frozen Mop, near Mobberley and The Greyhound at Ashley crossroads.

The Journey

Section a-b

Drop down out of the car park to a T-junction with a railway bridge going over the road to your right. Turn left and cycle along King Street. At the end of the high street you see the entrance to Tatton Park. Ride through the gateway and past the payment booth.

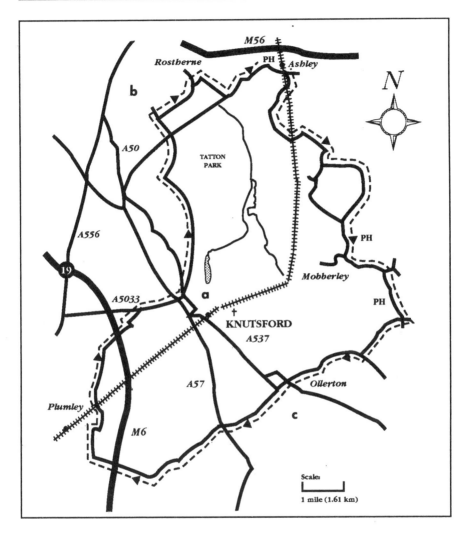

Cycle along the road through Tatton Park. You pass Tatton Mere to your right, a lake favoured by windsurfers and dinghy sailors, and you will see the Mansion across to the left through the trees.

After about a mile you cross a cattle grid, just after which the road forks. Carry straight on, up to another fork, where you follow the signs for the Rostherne exit. Cycle along the tree-lined avenue, out of the large black metal gates, to a road junction.

Go straight across, signposted to Rostherne and follow the road to the right. Take the first road on the right and cycle along, past a farm on the right, dropping down hill past Lower Marsh Cottages and climbing back up again. Follow the road to a fork, where you go right, signposted "Ashley, Hale, Wilmslow." Follow this around a sharp right-hand bend. Ride along, through the trees, around the left-hand bend and over the bridge. Keep going, over the railway bridge, and up to a crossroads at Ashley.

Section b-c

Go right at the crossroads, past Ashley Smithy Garage, through the right-hand bend and over the railway bridge. After around three-quarters of a mile, you pass a small green "Welcome to Mobberley" sign. Immediately after this, there are cottages to both sides of the road and, straight after these, you turn left down Breach House Lane.

Cycle over the bridge, under the railway, then all the way round to a T-junction. Go left then bear right, past Wood Lane. Pass Hill House on the right, a black and white building surrounded by trees. Bear right, past a road merging from the left. Keep straight on to a T-Junction. Go straight on, here, signed to Mobberley.

Follow the road to the left, past St Wilfred's Church on the right and Mobberley Primary School and The Church Inn Pub on the left. At a T-junction, go left, up Hall Lane. Take the first road on the right, Faulkners Lane, after just over half a mile. Soon, you cross a bridge and the Frozen Mop Pub on the right.

Continue along Faulkners Lane as it becomes Pedley House Lane, signed "Ollerton and Knutsford." You pass houses on the right and then Pedley House Farm. Keep straight on, towards Knutsford and Ollerton as Pedley House Lane becomes Marthall Lane. Soon, you enter Ollerton and reach a staggered crossroads with the A537.

Section c-a

At the crossroads with the A537, Chelford and Macclesfield are to the left, and Knutsford is to the right. Turn right, down Seven Sisters Lane, signposted to Lower Peover. Pass Manor Lane and go up to the T-junction.

Turn right, signposted to Knutsford and Warrington. 100 metres further down, turn first left on the B5081, signposted to Middlewich and Lower Peover. Lower Peover is about three-quarters of a mile from the junction. Keep straight on at the crossroads by the village green and go up to a second, staggered crossroads. Turn right along Plumley Moor Road.

Ride over the motorway and you'll pass a "Plumley, please drive slowly through the village" sign. At the crossroads, around a quarter of a mile from the motorway go right, signed "Knutsford". This is Pinfold Lane. Pass the houses on the left and right, and the road soon becomes Sudlow Lane and passes under a railway bridge. Cycle past Parkside Farm on the right, and cross over another motorway bridge further on.

At a T-junction with the A5033, go right, signposted to Macclesfield and Knutsford. Go straight across the first roundabout, signposted "Town Centre" and take the first right, Princess Street, past the Red Cow Pub. Cycle along , past the shops and up to a 'turn left only' T-junction. Cycle past Knutsford Civic Centre on the left, going left at a large crossroads with traffic lights. Drop down the hill, taking the first road on your left, King Street, under the railway bridge. The Station Car Park is first on the left.

29. Knutsford, Rostherne & Arley

Distance: 16 miles/22km.

Route: Knutsford entrance Tatton Park – Rostherne exit – Rostherne – Bucklow Hill – Hoo Green – Arley Green – Bate Heath – Tabley Hill – Knutsford – Knutsford entrance to Tatton Park.

Surface: Tarmac, gravel, grass and potentially muddy tracks

Start: Tatton Park (SJ745815).

Map: O.S. Landranger 109 (Manchester and surrounding area) and O.S. 118 (the Potteries).

The Route

The ride starts at the Knutsford entrance to Tatton Park. If you wish, you can use this route as an extension to those available from The National Trust office at Tatton. The Park has cycles for hire and is an excellent base for cycling with its woodlands, stately home, lakeland views and varied wildlife. The park is home to a number of deer.

From the Rostherne exit the route heads west to the village of Rostherne and then onto Bucklow Hill and Hoo Green. Arley Hall is an optional stop on this route, though access from the east is tricky by bike. After passing through Bate Heath the route leads you back over the M6 into Knutsford and Tatton Park. Refreshments are available at The Millers Kitchen, Hoo Green; The Swan, Bucklow Hill; The White Bear and The Red Cow, and many other pubs and cafes in Knutsford.

The Journey

Section a-b

If starting from Knutsford station, leave the main car park and turn left into King Street (Knutsford's main street). Ride to the end of it until you see the signs for Tatton Park. The park is on your right at this point.

From the Knutsford entrance to Tatton park, ride under the archway and through a small gate which avoids the cattlegrid. Continue past the warden's hut and follow the road ahead. After riding along Knutsford Drive, you pass Tatton Mere on the right and Melchet Mere on the left.

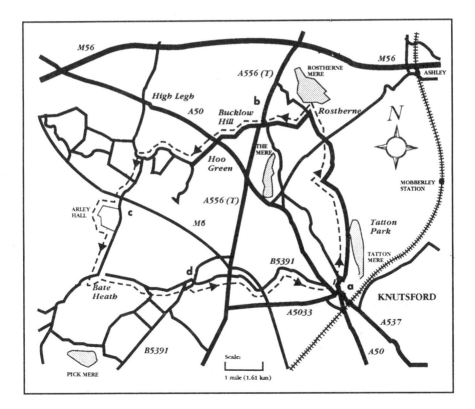

Follow Knutsford Drive until a fork in the road. Turn right, taking the sign for the Rostherne exit. This drive is tree-lined and deer are often seen in the woods.

At the Rostherne exit, beware of the cattle grids once again. Pass through the black gates and stop at the junction. Cross the road onto the lane opposite and follow the sign for Rostherne, a mile and a half away. Go half way through Rostherne village and take the first turn left. Ride uphill, follow the road ahead and drop down a steep hill, bearing right as the road goes further downhill.

On the left, there's an angler's pool and on the right a riding school. Ride over a small stream and continue up the other side of the hill along the small wooded lane. At the end of the lane, give way at the junction of the A5034.

On the right you'll see the Swan Inn. Turn right onto the A5034 and ride up to the traffic lights. Turn left at the lights onto the A556(T). Continue to the BP filling station. Dismount and cross this busy road with great care. Follow the lane opposite signed to Hoo Green (1 mile) and High Legh ($2^1/_2$ miles).

Section b-c

Ride for about a mile before sighting the pylons directly in front. Bear left around the bend and ride parallel to the pylons. Continue up to a junction with white metal fences.

Cross the A50 onto Hoo Green Lane. Drop downhill, and continue along the lane until you reach a junction. At the junction, turn left off Whiteley Lane and take the signs for Great Budworth, Pickmere and Arley Hall and Gardens. Ride over the M6 on Cann Lane and drop down after the bridge. Take the first right down a gravel path into the yard of Guidepost Farm.

Section c-d

Go through a rusty gate, closing it behind you. Continue along the gravel track which is popular with cyclists in the summer. The track has a mixture of surfaces. At the second gate, keep left and ride through the wood. Continue to a wooden gate which leads into a field, sloping away down a hill.

Turn left here and ride along the grass track with the farmhouse on the left. At the end of the track, turn right onto a tarmac lane. Ride down the hill and curve left onto cobble stones. Follow the lane over Arley Brook until reaching cottages.

From this point, Arley Hall and Gardens can be reached by foot (turn right and go up to the gate). To continue with the ride; turn left and follow the lane to the next junction. Turn right, go down the hill and then uphill past a stream and white fence on the left.

After about a mile, turn left at the next junction. There's a phone box on the right and a historic wall on the right which has the following words embossed upon a metal plaque:

THE PINFOLD, ASTON BY BUDWORTH. PROBABLY 18th CENTURY WALLS OF CYCLOPEAN, COWSED STONE. CHAMFERED COPING STONES WITH ADZE MARKS ON SIDES GIVING AN EFFECT OF VERNICULATED RUSTICATION.

A Pinfold, by the way, was an enclosure for stray cattle. How's that for a history lesson?

After turning off Cann Lane follow the signs for Tabley and Knutsford. Continue along Budworth Road, under the pylons and back towards Knutsford. Shortly after the pylons, bear sharp left. On the bend, ride over Arley Brook and up the hill. At the junction of the B5391, join the Cheshire Cycleway by turning left off Budworth Road.

Section d-a

After about half a mile you arrive at the A556(T) by junction 19 of the M6. The Windmill pub is on the left. Cross the A556(T), pass the filling station on the left and ride over the M6, under the pylons, and up Tabley Hill. After descending from Tabley Hill, follow the road into Knutsford's residential area. Continue along the A50 into Knutsford and back to your starting point.

30. Knutsford and Higher Peover

Distance: 13.5 miles/21.9km.

Route: Knutsford station – Higher Peover – Swan Green – Plumley – Knutsford station.

Surface: Tarmac with some hardcore and cobbles (easily passable, but if you do it on your best road bike you may feel slightly guilty afterwards).

Start: Knutsford station (SJ753784).

Map: O.S. 118 (the Potteries).

The Route

This route starts in historic Knutsford (700 years old in 1992) and Tatton Park (visited on other rides). The ride passes near to Peover Hall and Church used by US troops in the War (General Patton's flags fly in the Church, although it is now usually kept locked due to theft. The Hall is open to the public a few times a year).

Part of this route follows the A50 for around 4 km. This road is not usually very busy but it can be quite fast moving. There is an overlap with other Knutsford rides to avoid crossing the highly dangerous, motorway-like A556.

Refreshments: Whipping Stocks pub on the A50; Crown pub and village store at Swan Green; numerous places in Knutsford.

The Journey

Section a-b

Roll down out of the station car park, turn right and ride under the railway bridge and up to the T-junction. Turn right here and cycle up to the traffic lights, turning left onto the A50, signposted to Stoke-on-Trent. Keep cycling along the A50; after around 2 km you pass Toft Hall to your right.

Follow the signs for Holmes Chapel and cycle into Over Peover. About 4 km from the station, the A50 bends right and Stocks Lane goes off to the left. The Whipping Stocks pub is on the far side of Stocks Lane. Cycle past the entrance to Radbroke Hall on the left (owned by Barclays Bank) and ride into Over Peover village.

Section b-c

About 1.5 km from the A50, the road bends left and Grotto Lane goes off to the right (signposted Goostrey and Congleton). After half a kilometre, the road bends left and comes to a crossroads. Turn right here down the road opposite to Clay Lane (signposted to Goostrey).

Follow this road for a few hundred yards; it bends sharply left and you go right, through a white gateway signposted to Over Peover Church and Hall. Follow the speed-bumped road until you reach a three-way fork. Take the left-most road here, but first you may want to take a detour to have a quick look at the church. To do this, follow the signposts, go through the yard and past the out-buildings. The Hall was used by US forces in the Second World War, and General Patton's flags are still to be seen in the church, but you'll need to attend a service on a Sunday to see them.

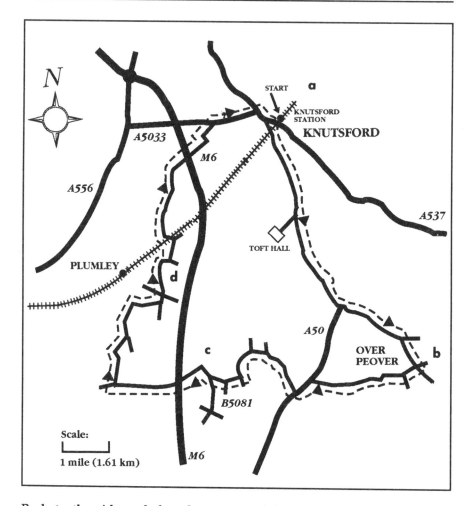

Back to the ride and that three-pronged fork. Go left at the fork, and follow the road until it bears sharply right. Here you ride in front of the two cottages and through a gateway. Cycle along the hardcore/cobbled track continuing through a gap in the fence towards a row of trees.

The track widens onto a gravel surface and, passing a large greenhouse on the left, becomes tarmac surfaced and tree-lined. Head towards, and past, the farm buildings directly in front. The road passes fields on either side, before curving left, and coming to a junction with the A50.

Ride left onto the A50, taking the first road on the right (Free Green Lane) signposted to Lower Peover. (Be careful here – the right hand turn is on a fast left-hand kink. Be sure that nothing is coming from the other direction before turning).

Follow Free Green Lane for about 1 km before rising up slightly through a wooded section, to be confronted by a Lower Peover sign. There are some houses on the right; turn left immediately before these down the narrow Mill Lane.

This lane ends at a T-junction with Foxcovert Lane, where you go left. Drop down the hill and cross the bridge over Peover Eye stream. Ride up the other side and follow the road around to the left. You pass a white house on the left (Brookfield House) and take the next right (a continuation of Foxcovert Lane).

Follow the lane to a T-junction with the B5081. Go right here riding into the 40mph zone and then turn left a few hundred metres further down into Hulme Lane, with the Crown pub on the corner.

Section c-d

Go through Swan Green village and cycle up and over the M6. Drop down the other side and, after a short distance, pass a row of houses on the right. Ignore the road going off to the right signed to Plumley, and continue for 1km before turning right into Patmos Lane (next right).

Continue along this lane, pass Moss Cottage until you reach a fork in the road. Go left, signed to Plumley, riding under the overhead cables. Continue to a T-junction, where you turn right, signed to Lower Peover. Ride past properties on the left and right and up to a T-junction after about 0.5 km. Turn off Trouthall Lane, signposted Lower Peover, and cycle up to a crossroads.

Section d-a

Go straight over into Pinfold Lane following it through a sharp right in front of Woods Tenement Farm, about 0.5 km from a crossroads and through the left-hand bend immediately afterwards.

Continue riding, following signs for Knutsford, and passing under the railway line just after the road becomes Swallow Lane. You pass Parkside Nursery on the right after a short distance, and eventually pass over the M6 again. (Knutsford services can be seen on the left).

The road bends left before twisting sharply right in front of Swallow Farm. About 0.5 km later, you reach a T-junction with the A5033. Turn right, signposted to Macclesfield and Knutsford.

After about 1 km, you reach a roundabout. Go right, signposted to Stoke, Macclesfield and the Station. Cycle through the first set of traffic lights, past a second set of lights (Pelican crossing) and up to a major junction with 'real' traffic lights. Here you can either carry your bike down the steps to the station, or turn left at the lights, drop down the hill and take the first road on the left..

31. Lymm to High Legh

Distance: 23 miles/37km.

Route: Queen Victoria Memorial – Grappenhall – Appleton Thorn – Stretton – Lower Stretton – Antrobus Hall – Swarton Heath – High Legh – Broom Edge – Heatley – Queen Victoria Memorial.

Surface: Tarmac, cobblestones, concrete.

Start: Queen Victoria Memorial in Lymm town centre (SK683873).

Map: O.S. Landranger 109 (Manchester and surrounding area).

The Route

The route starts from the Queen Victoria Memorial in the centre of Lymm and heads west under the M6 towards Warrington. At Grappenhall we travel south to Appleton Thorn and onwards to Stretton. After crossing the M56 the route winds its way along secluded country lanes. At one point, it travels along a disused airfield and a taxiway makes up a section of the lane!

The journey returns over the M6 and onwards to Swarton Heath. From Swarton Heath you pass High Legh and onto Broomedge along the B5159 to join up with the A6144 which takes you back to the centre of Lymm. Refreshments are easy to find, try: the Golden Fleece, Lymm; the Parr Arms and the Rams Head, Grappenhall; the Thorn, Appleton Thorn; the Cat & Lion pub, Stretton.

The journey

Section a-b

Start at the Queen Victoria Memorial, which commemorates her diamond jubilee in 1897. On the opposite side of the road up the hill is the Golden Fleece pub. Do not ride up that way – instead, turn left onto the A6144 and ride over the pelican crossing. (*Pedestrian Light Controlled Crossing*, almost an acronym for Pelican)

Follow the road round to the right. Travel over the Bridgewater Canal, past the Spread Eagle Hotel on the left and onwards up the hill. Continue along the road and over the mini roundabout until the A56 is reached. Turn right at the junction onto the A56.

Follow the road ahead until you reach a Jet petrol station on the right. Opposite the station is Massey Brook Lane. Turn left here and continue down the lane, riding parallel to the Bridgewater Canal as you go. Ride under the M6 motorway and continue to the end of the lane. Turn right onto Cliff Lane and ride along the cobbled surface through the narrow tunnel under the canal.

Follow Cliff Lane round to the left until reaching the A50. Turn right onto the A50 and immediately after, take the first left onto Bellhouse Lane and ride towards Grappenhall.

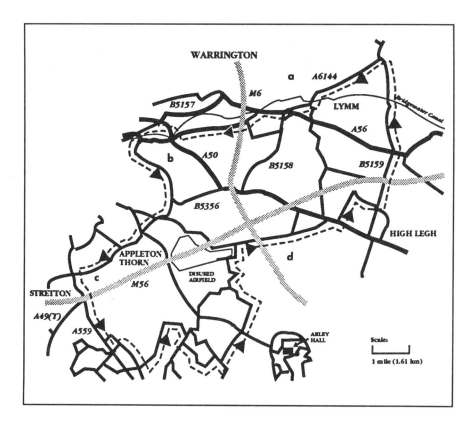

Section b-c

Follow the road ahead into Grappenhall riding over the hump-backed bridge, this time crossing above the Bridgewater Canal. Continue along the cobbled road past St Wilfred's Church and the Parr Arms, both of which are on the right.

Follow the road ahead past the Ram's Head pub and up to the junction. Turn left at the junction onto Broad Lane. Ride up the hill and onwards along the lane. The view behind is especially impressive at night with the lights of Warrington and the Greater Manchester area filling the horizon.

Follow the road ahead to a roundabout. At the roundabout take the second exit and follow the signs for Stretton on the B5356. A few hundred metres up the road take the first right and continue following signs for Stretton.

Ride through Appleton Thorn with the Thorn pub on the right as you pass through. Just over a mile along the road, ride into Stretton and stop at the traffic lights. From here turn left off the Stretton road (B5356) and onto the A559.

Section c-d

At a large roundabout take the second exit down the A559. Ride past the Ring of Bells pub on the left. Follow the A559 ahead until reaching the Birch and Bottle pub, where you turn left and ride down an unsigned lane.

At the end of the lane, turn right onto Foggs Lane. At the end of this lane, turn left and follow the lane past Antrobus Hall until it reaches a sharp bend to the right. Follow it around until it again bends right. Follow Reed Lane ahead until reaching the junction. Turn right here and follow the road ahead until you reach Nook Lane which is the first lane on your left.

Continue to the end of what is now Flash Lane. Turn right onto Pools Plat Lane. Nearly immediately after, take another left onto Lodge Lane. Follow the road ahead, ride over Arley Brook and continue along the lane. On reaching the crossroads, ride across the junction and follow the signs for Sandilands.

Follow this tarmac lane ahead, as it winds left and right. At the junction near Reedgate Farm bear right. Continue along the lane until reaching a taxiway which is part of a disused airfield and which has been incorporated as part of the lane. The taxiway is very wide and can cause confusion after arriving from a narrow country lane, so keep to the left.

After leaving the taxiway, ride to the end of the unsigned lane, which the route now follows.

Section d-a

Ride to the end of the lane. Turn right at the junction and follow the signs for High Legh. The road continues towards Swarton Heath and over the M6 motorway.

At Swarton Heath turn right onto the A50. Ride up the road to the Bear's Paw Inn. Just after this, turn left into Crab Tree Lane and take the very sharp right turn a few hundred metres down the lane.

Continuing on from Crab Tree Lane is Old Pen Brow. Turn left at the end of this lane away from High Legh and onto the B5159. Follow the road ahead over the M56 and onwards to Broom Edge. At Broom Edge, ride through the traffic lights and continue along the B5159.

Ride under the Bridgewater Canal and on towards the A6144. Just before the A6144 is a disused level crossing. By this crossing is The Railway pub, used in the 'Families' television drama produced by Granada TV.

On reaching the A6144 turn left at the junction and follow the road ahead. Ride over the Bridgewater Canal and down the hill, finally to arrive back in the centre of Lymm by Queen Victoria's Memorial.

32. Lymm and Dunham

Distance: 11.5 miles/18km.

Route: Lymm – Oughtrington – Mossbrow – Dunham Town – Dunham Park – Booth Bank – Deansgreen – Lymm.

Surface: Tarmac, hardcore, shale.

Start: Lymm town centre (SK683873).

Map: O.S. Landranger 109 (Manchester and surrounding area).

The Route

This 11 mile ride is one which could be tackled by almost anyone. It doesn't include any major hills as the terrain in and around Lymm is very flat. There are only two off-road sections on the route, as there are hardly any bridleways in this area. This also means that the route travels on some main roads, so if children are going to attempt this ride, be careful. The ancient cross in the centre of Lymm carries a weather vane and sundials on each of its four sides. There's also a set of stocks at the foot of the cross. Dunham Park is a picturesque park owned by the National Trust, and the home and gardens are well worth a visit. However, bicycles are not allowed in the grounds, so to visit the park you would be well advised to take a strong lock. There are two car parks at Dunham Park; a large pay car park (start of second section) and a small free car park further down the road (shown in map).

There are six pubs on the route, any of which would be a good place to stop for a well-earned break.

The Journey

Section a-b

From the free car park on Pepper Street adjacent to the old cross, turn left up the cobbled street. Soon the road becomes a tarmac surface and continues into a bridleway (marked Oughtrington 1km); follow this track which runs next to the Bridgewater Canal. At the end of the track, turn left over a hump-backed bridge (TAKE CARE) and follow the road round to the right.

Fork right onto Stage Lane. Turn left at the traffic lights, eventually crossing a disused railway line. Continue until you reach the A6144 and the Green Dragon, turn right here.

Follow the main road for about a mile, passing the Saracen's Head pub and a church. Then, turn right following signs for Altrincham and Dunham, down Dunham Road (B5160). Turn left after about a mile at the Rope and Anchor, then immediately right down Back Lane.

This road crosses the Bridgewater Canal and shortly reaches a T-junction. Turn right into School Lane which becomes Woodhouse Lane, as you pass a tree stump in the middle of the junction. At the end of the road, turn right along the edge of Dunham Park with the wall of the park on your left. Follow this for half a mile until you reach the car park. There is a parking fee, so take advantage of this to lock and leave your bike and visit Dunham Park.

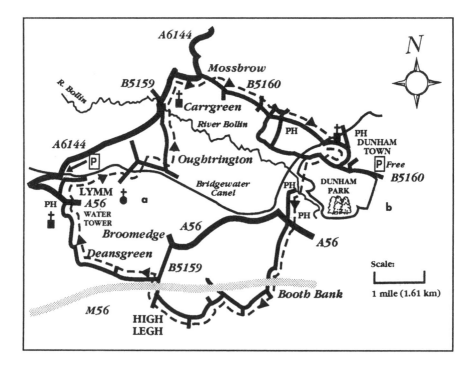

Section b-a

From the car park turn left (B5160) and take the next left down a shale track signed Bollington Mill. At the end of the track carry your bike over

the narrow bridge (River Bollin) and continue past the 'Swan with Two Nicks' – not a mis-print, but a reference to the ancient method of denoting swan ownership. Follow the road round to the left and up to the T-junction, with the Stamford Arms pub in your left.

Turn left here, then immediately right down Reddy Lane. Continue under the M56 and fork right, following the signs to High Legh and Lymm up Booth Bank Lane. Keep to this road and take the second left before a thatched cottage on Moss Lane. At the end of this road, turn right down Peacock Lane, eventually reaching a crossroads. Turn right here (B5159).

The 'Swan with Two Nicks'

Follow the road over the motorway and take the next left turn down Beechtree Lane. Follow this road for two miles and eventually arrive in Lymm. Turn left here onto the A56 and take the next right down Rectory Lane opposite the Church Green pub. Follow this down past The Dingle House Hotel on the left and, at the bottom of the road, is Lymm Cross where you turn right for Pepper Street and the free car park.

33. Macclesfield to Gawsworth

Distance: 20 miles/32km

Route: Macclesfield Station – Bailey Ridding – Warren – Gawsworth Hall – Marton – Hodgehill – Redesmere – Fanshawe – Lower Pexhill – Broken Cross – Macclesfield Station.

Surface: Tarmac and bridleways.

Start: Macclesfield Railway Station (SJ920736).

Map: O.S. 118 (the Potteries).

The Route

This route is fairly lengthy and, with some busy main roads and a number of hill climbs, it is not advised for unaccompanied youngsters. Some of the off-road tracks are fairly bumpy, so care is needed.

There are five pubs *en route* and there are plenty of places in Macclesfield where you can buy food and drink for a packed lunch.

The start of this route is Macclesfield railway station. There are two other possible start points: Gawsworth Hall and Capesthorne Hall. If you travel to Capesthorne by car there is an entrance fee, but at Gawsworth there is adequate parking on by-roads near the hall. Both of these halls are well worth visiting both for their interiors and the surrounding gardens.

The Journey

Section a-b

Leave Macclesfield railway station and turn left, following the road through part of the shopping area. At the traffic lights go straight ahead onto Park Street. Cycle up to a roundabout and take the road to your left – Park Lane. Stay on this road until you reach the first set of traffic lights after Macclesfield College.

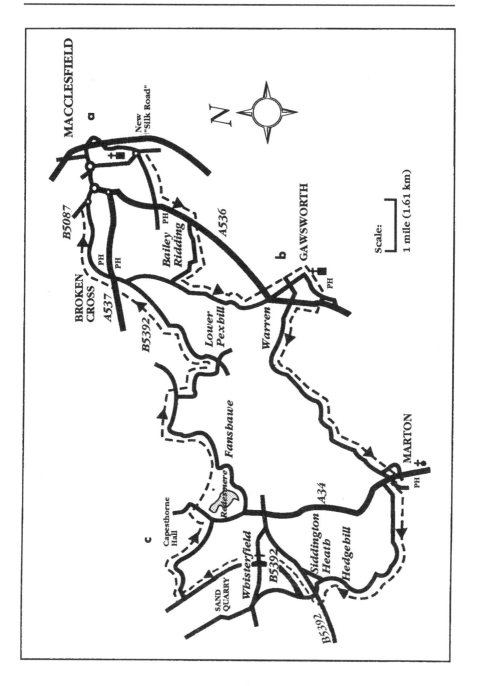

Turn left here and continue past the Flower Pot pub on your right, and
the Texaco garage on your left. Take the first right turning after the garage onto Pennington's Lane. Soon this road becomes a track which
leads up to Bailey Riddings farm. Go down the track and, at the farm,
follow it round to the left.

At the end of the track, cycle onto the road and turn left. At the end of
this road – Gawsworth Road – you come out at Dark Lane. Turn left
here and continue up to the crossroads, at the A536, go straight across
this main road onto Church Lane, taking your next right to Gawsworth
Hall.

Section b-c

To leave Gawsworth Hall turn right and cycle past the ponds on your
left. Stay on this road and you will soon see the Harrington Arms. Turn
right before the pub and continue until you reach the main road. Turn
right again and then turn left onto Marton Lane. Keep on this road for
about two miles, cycling past Mill House farm and Tidnock Woods on
your left.

After Marton Heath church, cycle along School Lane and up to a
T-junction. Turn right here and then take an immediate left after the
garage into Davenport Lane. Continue past two farms on either side of
the road to a junction at Hodge Hill Lane. Turn right and follow the
road until it forks. Take the left fork and continue to a crossroads,
where you go straight across onto Chapel Lane.

*As with Route 3, quarry workings in Lapwing Lane have caused a
change in this route, which is now as follows:* Continue along Chapel
Lane for 200 metres and then fork right along Moss Lane. At the end of
Moss Lane (three-quarters of a mile) turn left and, after just 100 metres,
keep right along Chelford Road. Continue for a mile and a quarter,
then turn right into Mill Lane. Continue along this narrow lane, cross a
bridge and, at the very end, turn left onto the A34. Continue from here
to the main entrance of Capesthorne Hall.

Section c-a

In the interests of your safety, we have deliberately taken you past the
turn that you needed! So, from the entrance to Capesthorne Hall, cross
the A34 *(probably safer to push your bike across the road)* turn right and

head back the way you have just cycled in on the A34. At a right-hand bend, turn left onto a bridleway – this is the safe way to do it: much better than trying to turn right across the A34! Go through the gate and onto a stony track with the sailing club on your right. Do not follow the track round to the left, but go straight on over to the gate. Go through the gate and continue over a stream up to a left turn. Turn here onto a grassy area and then take a right turn onto a narrow road.

At the end of this road turn left and continue for about 1.5 miles, cycling past Fanshawe Brook Farm and up to Bearhurst Lane. Turn right here and, at the end, turn left onto the B5392. Follow this road all the way down to a T-junction where you turn left. Continue up to and across a roundabout with the Bull's Head pub opposite, onto Fallibroome Road. You will soon reach another roundabout, which you cross onto Priory Lane. Cycle past Parkside Hospital and Macclesfield General on your right to another small roundabout. Turn right here and head to the first of five roundabouts which will take you back to the station – through Macclesfield's "improved" road system.

Redesmere, near to Capesthorne Hall and a welcome picnic spot

34. Macclesfield Forest

Distance: 6 miles/10km

Route: Visitor Centre – Forest Chapel – Teggs Nose Reservoir – Langley – Visitor Centre

Surface: Tarmac, stones and rocks!.

Start Point: Macclesfield Forest Visitor Centre (SJ965716)

Map: O.S. 118 (the Potteries).

The Route

This is a short but steep and rugged route around Macclesfield Forest, including a visit to Forest Chapel and using tracks and paths inaccessible by car. The area is popular with mountain bikers (some of whom have been known to stray into North West Water's property). The combination of steep hills and stony surfaces will soon persuade you to use a mountain bike; the surface really is too rough for racing bikes, but with a normal 'tourer' you should manage most of it with low gears and strong legs. In any case, the steep parts are pleasant walks!

There are two pubs on the route, The Setter Dog and The Leathers Smithy.

The Journey

Section a-b

If starting from Macclesfield Station . . .

This adds about three miles to get to the start point: leave the station and turn left to the traffic lights, then turn left again along Leek Road. Go through the next set of traffic lights and after half a mile, turn left up Byrons Lane, signposted Sutton, Langley and Wincle. After the Old Kings Head turn left up Jarman, following the signs to Langley. The road climbs gradually through Langley to the Leathers Smithy where it bears to the right, past Ridgegate Reservoir on the right. Keep to this road (ignore the minor road to the right) and the Macclesfield Forest Visitor Centre is about half a mile up the hill on the right-hand side.

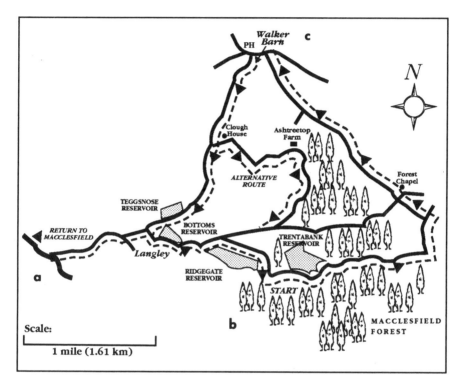

Section b-c

From the Visitor Centre . . .

Turn right from the Visitor Centre and ride alongside Trentabank Reservoir on your left. Be sure to stop in the lay-by and do a bit of bird-spotting; across the reservoir, herons are often seen and there is a display board to help non-ornithologists. From here, the road gets much steeper, but even if you have to walk, it's a pleasant – almost Alpine – stroll.

At the top of the hill, turn left. From this high-level lane, there are great views to your right, with The Cat and Fiddle on the horizon and

Wildboarclough nestling below. Follow the road for a few hundred yards, take the first left turn and again climb steeply towards Forest Chapel.

At the next junction, you'll be going straight ahead (with a "dead end" sign facing you). But take the opportunity to visit Macclesfield Forest Chapel (St Stephen's); this is a peaceful place, renowned for the hundreds of varieties of plants in its grounds.

Back to the ride: go straight on at the crossroads up an increasingly-steep and rough track. At the end of the track turn right onto a well-surfaced lane. TAKE EXTREME CARE as this goes downhill very steeply and there is a busy main road (the A537) at the end of it. Turn left at the T-junction and go downhill towards the Setter Dog. Just before the pub, take the *first* turn left, signed Crooked Yard Farm. Be sure not to overshoot and take the second left, which leads to Teggs Nose country park.

Section c-a/b

This road drops downhill; it's narrow and steep and you may meet the odd car from the farms so go carefully and be sure that you can stop quickly. Pass a farm track on the left, drop into the valley and, if you can spare the time, admire Croker Hill in the distance and Shutlingsloe to the left. At Clough House Farm, you have a choice:

The almost-impossible route:

Turn left, signposted "Forest Chapel". At first, this seems quite promising but as you pass Crooked Yard Farm, the going gets tougher. No mountain bike, no go! North West Water own this track and the surrounding land and have allowed access by foot or bike. Perhaps if some public-spirited person could remove the obstructing rocks or if the water authorities would let us have some better tracks?

To struggle onwards, dip downhill, cross a stream and then head uphill. After a few more hundred yards, the track turns left. You pass Hardingland and then Ashtreetop farm on your left; the track bears right then left and finally swings right to head downhill through the forest and down to a tarmac lane. Turn right here, and go downhill to The Leathers Smithy; from here, either turn right to return to Macclesfield or left to return to the Visitor Centre.

The just-about-possible route

At Clough House Farm, turn right onto a bridleway with Teggs Nose above you on the right. Go through a few gates and over a stream, until you come to A T-junction with a better-surfaced track. Turn right, with a stream on your right, and follow the track until you reach Teggs Nose Reservoir. Here the track ends and becomes a tarmac road (Holehouse Lane). At the end of this road either turn right to return to Macclesfield or turn left and, after passing the Leathers Smithy, keep to the road past Ridgegate Reservoir and return to the Visitor Centre.

Note: the above reflects the situation as at January 1993. It is possible that North West Water may, sometime in the future, permit cycling on certain routes only open to pedestrians at present. Check the current situation at The Visitor Centre.

35. Macclesfield and Wildboarclough

Distance: 15 miles/24km.

Route: Macclesfield Station – Sutton – Wincle – Wildboarclough – Teggs Nose – Macclesfield Station.

Surface: Tarmac.

Start: Macclesfield Railway Station (SJ920736).

Map: O.S. 118 (the Potteries).

The Route

This route is 15 miles long and very strenuous, although it may be tackled on a road bike, as the route never strays from tarmac roads. There are several pubs including the Crag Inn in Wildboarclough. This pub is next to Clough Brook which was the scene of a major catastrophe on 24 May 1989. During a severe storm, there was a build-up of water at the head of the valley; an embankment broke under the weight of the water, releasing a sudden flood which smashed walls, uprooted trees, swept away bridges and ripped up parts of the road surface. The whole valley has now been restored and it is hard to imagine how such a small brook could be capable of such devastation.

This route is particularly good for its views of Macclesfield and the Cheshire plains, the Roaches, Macclesfield Forest, Shutlingsloe and Wildboarclough.

The Journey

Section a-b

Leave the station, turn left to the traffic lights and then left along Leek Road. Go through the next set of traffic lights and, after half a mile, turn left up Byrons Lane, signposted to Sutton, Langley and Wincle. Follow signs for Sutton and continue gradually uphill for 3 miles, passing the Ryles Arms part-way along this pleasant road. Eventually you join the A54 where you turn left, continuing to climb for a quarter of a mile and, at the crossroads, turn right towards Wincle.

From here, there are impressive views to the left of the jagged outline of the Roaches and, to the right, Croker Hill's microwave tower is an impressive landmark. About half a mile down the road towards Wincle, take the first right down a narrow track, through a series of gates and cattlegrids; at the end of this road, turn left and, when you reach Wincle church, turn right following the signs for Wildboarclough. Climb uphill past Hill Top Farm and then downhill to the A54 and straight across at the crossroads (TAKE CARE). Follow this road, climbing gradually into Wildboarclough, with Clough Brook on your right.

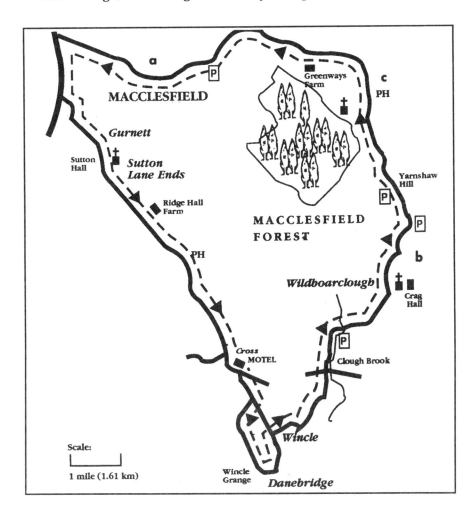

Section b-c

The Crag Inn is reached eventually (car parks both before and after the pub) and you might like to stop at this friendly refreshment post. Continuing ever-onward, at the end of this road you reach the Stanley Arms; turn left in front of the pub and climb up the hill for half a mile and take the first left turn. Follow this road with the Macclesfield-Buxton (A537) road about 200 yards away on your right. The road soon joins the A537; turn left here and follow it to the Setter Dog Pub.

Section c-a

(If starting from the Setter Dog, note that there is limited parking: ask the publican before using the pub car park.)

Turn left just before the pub, with signs to Teggs Nose country park. At popular times, you can get refreshments from the kiosk at the information centre. From Teggs Nose, follow the road for a mile and a half steeply downhill and join the A537 again, turning left onto it. Continue all the way down the A537 and through the traffic lights at the bottom of the hill. Go straight on under the railway line, turn left at the roundabout and the station is on your left.

Devastation in 1989 – remains of a bridge in Wildboarclough

36. Macclesfield to Whaley Bridge – the hard way!

Distance: 19 miles/30km.

Route: Macclesfield – Rainow – Blue Boar Farm – Jenkin Chapel – Taxal Edge – Fernilee Reservoir – Whaley Bridge – Kettleshulme – Rainow – Macclesfield.

Surface: Tarmac, grass and cinder, rock and mud (the latter is optional).

Start: Macclesfield Railway Station (SJ920736).

Map: O.S. 118 (the Potteries) and O.S. 110 (Sheffield and Huddersfield area).

The Route

This circular, long-distance ride is exhilarating, challenging and not for the faint-hearted. Families with small children would probably enjoy it more from the comfort of the car. Some of the most rugged and spectacular scenery of east Cheshire and Derbyshire as it borders the Pennine chain will be encountered.

A full day (5 – 6 hours) should be allowed to include ample time for stopping, leg-stretching and tea-shop-visiting. There are many pubs *en route* out of and into Macclesfield, Rainow and Whaley Bridge, but the Tea Cosy in Kettleshulme is highly recommended for a filling and wholesome tea (strange opening hours – telephone and check 01663 732116). Once into drystone wall land above Rainow there are many testing climbs and eye-watering descents. On a clear day you can see for ever, on a wet day you'll see nothing, though you may hear damp sheep bleat through the mist.

For convenience the ride starts at Macclesfield station. Your desire to climb (literally) above Macclesfield and its suburbs will breed the determination necessary for the rest of the ride! Rainow is a slightly softer option as a starting point.

The Journey

Section a-b

Leave the station and turn right onto the A537. At the traffic island follow the road under the railway line, turning immediately left onto the A523 (Stockport and Manchester). At the next roundabout (opposite Tesco) take the last exit on the right (Chapel-en-le-Frith and Whaley Bridge). Watch out for the Tesco slip-road on the left. Don't take it, but climb for 1 mile, crossing the canal, to the phone box on the right in Higher Hurdsfield at the bottom of Cliff Lane. For those who fancy a tougher challenge, or a change from the main road, turn right up Cliff Lane, and second left down into Calrofold to rejoin the B5470 just below Rainow. Turn right.

Continue the climb. Notice, in 50 yards on the left, a steep lane coming off the end of another challenging ride from Bollington along the saddle of Kerridge. Continue through Rainow, passing the Robin Hood and Rising Sun Inns. Drop down past a pretty pint cottage on the left, notice the cat and dove on the porch roof, and climb up past Rainow parish church and, at the end of the village, the chapel. In half a mile, turn right up innocuously named Smith Lane. We are now in the wide open upland on the fringe of the Peak District. Few gradients in this area are less than 1:10, so this is good practice and I usually walk it.

Turn right at the T-junction and pass Blue Boar Farm on the left. Immediately beyond the farm on the left there is an opportunity to carry your bike for 1 mile over rocks and mud. Some people enjoy this, though it stretches my definition of cycling. It is not for the timorous and is, in my opinion, unridable. However, ahead of me amongst the rocks and raging torrents were the tyre tracks of ones who had gone before. As I didn't find them, they presumably got through or were picked to pieces by vultures long ago. This rutted diversion reverts to cobbles and finally tarmac to rejoin the main route at Jenkin chapel (dated 1733).

A further climb (1:6 approx) of $^3/_4$ mile brings you to Taxal Edge. The main route plunges on to the Goyt Valley (1 mile). Those of sound mind will turn left here (Kettleshulme 2 miles) and descend passing Windgather Rocks, festooned with climbers on a fine day, and a favourite spot for hang gliders, to wait for us in the Tea Cosy at the bottom.

Section b-c

The main route descends between elegant beech and larch to the dam between the Errwood and Fernilee reservoirs. Cross the dam (Buxton 4

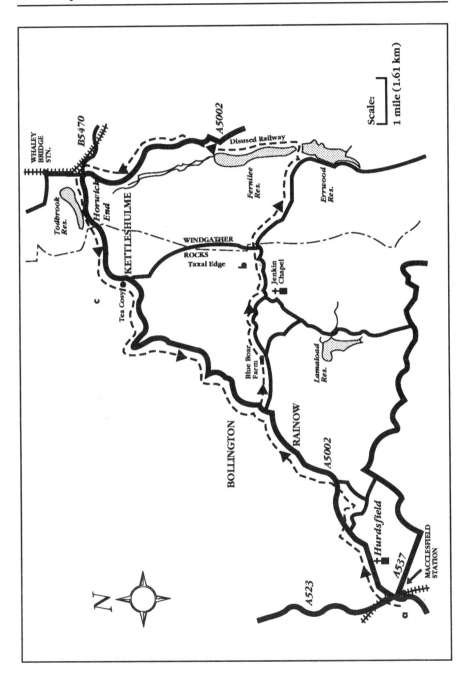

miles, toilets up the hill) and turn immediately left under the white barrier to join the disused railway track which runs for 1 mile along the side of Fernilee reservoir. You'll have to lift your bike over stiles at each end of this flat stretch (yes, flat!) but it is a pleasant and tranquil ride.

At the end of the track bear right and climb through woodland to join the Buxton – Whaley Bridge road (A5004). Turn left and pedal hard into Whaley Bridge (singularly grim on a wet day) and turn left onto the Macclesfield Road (B5470) at the main crossroads. Continue for 2 miles to Kettleshulme. The road down from Windgather Rocks appears on the left. The Tea Cosy is on the right. (Those who, very sensibly, avoided the Goyt Valley experience, will be in there looking warm, comfortable and well-fed and you'll hate them for it – let them buy you tea and you'll feel better!).

Section c-a

From here back to Macclesfield is 7 miles of plain sailing. Follow the B5470 and turn left at the Tesco roundabout on the A523. Turn right under the railway line and left at the island. The station is on the left.

Yes, there are easier ways of spending a Sunday, but few will give you such a sense of achievement. Well done!

The Tea Cosy – highly recommended!

37. Nantwich, south-bound

Distance: 10 miles/16km.

Route: Nantwich Station – Shropshire Union Canal – Edleston Farm – Stonely Green – Swanley Hall – Ravensmoore – Sound – Newtown – Mickley Hall – Hack Green – Nantwich Station.

Surface: Tarmac.

Start: Nantwich Railway Station (SJ653519).

Map: O.S. 118 (the Potteries).

The Route

The route leaves Nantwich Station and skirts the south-west edge of the town. We cycle west over the Shropshire Union Canal and towards the Windmill at Acton.

From here, the route travels south through the villages of Ravensmoor, Sound and Newtown. Finally, head north through Hack Green, past Nantwich Lake, to Nantwich Railway Station.

The Journey

Section a-b

From Nantwich Station, ride along the A529 towards the Town Centre. Take the first exit from the roundabout and follow the signs for Wrexham on the A534. Follow the ring road past the pedestrian crossing to a set of traffic lights, turn left and cross the bridge over the River Weaver. There are numerous pubs on the left and right of this road out of Nantwich.

After passing the Burmah Petrol Station on the right, take the first left up Marsh Lane. Follow the road ahead, past the estate on the left. The road takes a sharp bend to the right. Follow this bend which is signposted for Wrenbury and which also goes over on the Shropshire Union Canal. Continue along this road for a few hundred metres to the second turning right, Tally Ho Lane. Ride down this lane and follow the route ahead. The road surface here is very rough and could be treacherous when wet. On reaching the crossroads at Dig Lane, carry on straight ahead from Madams Farm; Acton Church can be seen across the fields.

Section b-c

At the end of Tally Ho Lane, note the disused windmill which lies north across the fields. At the junction, turn left and follow the sign for Wrenbury down Swanley Lane. At the end of this lane is a bridge which runs over the canal. Avoid this and turn left down the continuation of Swanley Lane, again signposted for Wrenbury. Ride south past Stoneley Green and towards Ravensmoor. On entering Ravensmoor there is a general store on the left and a few hundred metres away, the Farmer's Arms.

Ride straight ahead across the junction to Sound Lane and follow the route ahead. The lane curves left and then over the main Crewe-Shrewsbury rail line. After entering Sound Village, bear left and follow the signs for Nantwich. The lane leads to Newtown.

Section c-d

Leave the lane at Newtown and turn right onto the A530. A few hundred metres along this road, turn left into Heatley Lane. Approximately 100 metres up the lane, turn left again and after almost a mile, take a sharp left. Follow the lane ahead, ride over the Shropshire Union Canal once again and onwards towards Hock Green.

Section d-a

At the junction in Hack Green, turn left for Nantwich and ride along the lane. Approximately a mile from the junction are Old Hall Austerson Houses. Carry straight on, and the lane eventually meets up with the A530. From here, turn right and ride back towards Nantwich. Soon, on the left, is Nantwich Lake, an ideal spot for a picnic before riding back to the station. Follow the A530 after leaving Nantwich Lake to a junction

where you turn left onto the A529 (Wellington Road) and head back to
the Railway Station.

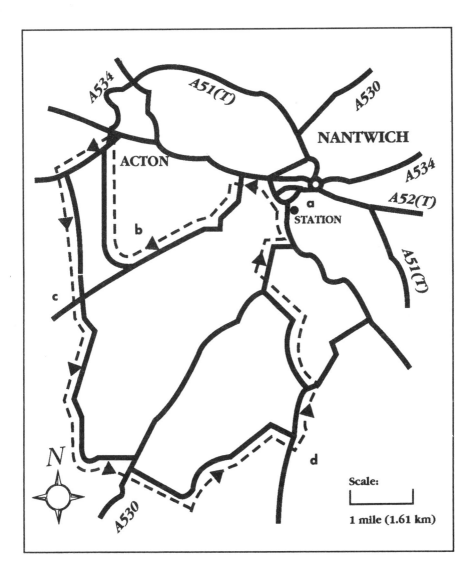

38. Nantwich and Cholmondeley

Distance: 22 Miles/35km

Route: Nantwich – Acton – Larden Green – Chorley – Cholmondeley Castle – Hetherson Green – Bickley Moss – Marbury – Marley Green – Wrenbury – Wrenbury Heath – Ravensmoor – Nantwich

Surface: Tarmac

Map: O.S. 117 (Chester) and O.S. 118 (the Potteries).

Start: Nantwich Railway Station (SJ654519)

The Route

This fairly easy ride strikes out from the unspoilt gem that is Nantwich into the gently undulating countryside between the town and the Shropshire border – a corner of Cheshire that is very much 'mere' country. In exploring this area, the route takes in a number of enchanting villages, one of the county's finest old houses, a castle (of the nineteenth century variety) with its superior gardens, windmills, canals and of course Nantwich itself. What more could you want?

Getting from A to B to C along the route should only take two and a half to three hours in itself but what with Dorfold Hall, Cholmondeley Castle gardens and every one of the numerous pubs along the route being open to the public a further couple of hours could easily be swallowed up. With regards to the first two, if you plan to visit these it is well worth checking in advance the opening times so that your ride won't be a disappointment. A cautionary note: the lanes, particularly between Cholmondeley Castle and Marbury are maze-like so it pays to follow the directions closely and/or consult the map. Doing so, you'd be hard-pressed to manage to get lost.

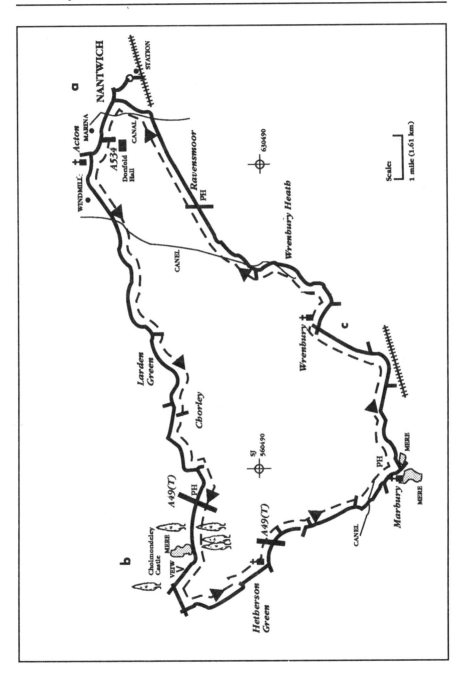

The Journey

Section a-b

For a town of its size, Nantwich has been bestowed with a very humble railway station. For those not arriving by train, there is more ample car parking signposted from the route a few hundred yards in. Heading north towards the town from the station, you are immediately confronted with a roundabout at which you should bear left down towards the River Weaver.

On reaching the traffic lights, turn left over the seventeenth century bridge and head up along Welsh Row – so called because it was along here that the Welsh farmers would drive their cattle to trade for the salt that would see them through the long winter months. Passing under the aqueduct and out into the south Cheshire countryside, off to your right is a marina (complete with gift shop!) and away to the left is Dorfold Hall. Open to the public, this 17th century symmetrical brick building is a charming example of the architectural fashion of its time.

An ancient tree in the grounds of Dorfold Hall is said to mark the southern limit of the old forest of Delamere, a history reflected further in Acton, meaning 'the settlement in the oaks', the village which is soon reached. Passing the Star turn left down the narrow lane immediately before the red sandstone church. The magnificent church at Nantwich was once but a chapel of ease to this and it also lays claim to having the oldest church tower in Cheshire. Forking off left and then continuing in the same direction along the road you swiftly join, you can see away to the right a sizeable windmill now sadly bereft of its sails but with much of its mechanics still intact and on view.

Continue for some five miles along this lane, over the Llangollen Branch of the Shropshire Union Canal, through Larden Green and Chorley, until you find yourself cycling up to a T- junction. Turn right and, upon reaching the Cholmondeley Arms, cross the A49(T) to head for Cholmondeley Castle. Passing a quaint thatched Gamekeeper's cottage and amongst that rarest of things – a non-coniferous wood – you'll soon see, away to the right, first a sizeable mere and then the imposing castle in whose parklands it lies. Actually more a house than a castle, the present building was completed very early in the nineteenth century in an imitation 'gothick' style. Cholmondeley Castle, however, is better known for its gardens which are open to the public and its attendant chapel which predates the 'castle' itself. The former, if you're at all horticulturally inclined, makes for compulsory viewing if you manage to time your visit right.

Section b-c

Returning to our route, turn left off the lane opposite the impressive entrance to the grounds of the castle and left again to head for Hetherson Green. A sharp right turn then takes you past a converted chapel to another T-junction. Turning left and then immediately right to head for Bickley, you'll find yourself approaching the delightful church of St Wenefredes with its charming gatehouse flanked by two huge plump conifers. Carrying on past it brings you to another T-junction – turn left and on reaching the A49(T) you should carefully continue straight across and then bear right to head south for Marbury. As you join another lane, head in the same direction, up the hill and across a nasty hump-backed bridge over the canal until you find yourself in what proudly proclaims itself as a regular winner of the Best Kept Village award. Turn left down past (if you can manage it!) the Swan which stands opposite one of the two meres from which the town draws its name. From the village green you can look up to the fifteenth century church of St Michael beautifully situated above the largest of the meres.

Keeping on along the lane into which you have just turned, bear left until you find yourself in Wrenbury, a now sizeable village that retains its charm by dint of the old squat church by the village green and the tiny post office-cum-village stores. Turning right and cycling past the village green and the surprisingly architecturally sophisticated primary school, you find yourself on the lane that will take you the six miles back to Nantwich. In doing so, you'll pass through Wrenbury Heath, cross and re-cross the Llangollen branch of the Shropshire Union Canal, pass through Ravensmoor – most notable for the Farmers' Arms and over the sort of hump-backed bridge you could take off from, had you the strength or inclination to be bothered to do so! Once over the bridge, follow the road round to the left and through all its twists and turns until you once again find yourself on Welsh Row from whence you should retrace your route to round off the day's cycling.

Section c-a

However, once past the bridge, if you were to cycle straight on at the traffic lights you would find yourself in Nantwich's elegant town centre. Once only second to Chester in importance, it is home to what some, admittedly usually guide-book writers, call the cathedral of south Cheshire, with good cause. One of the finest medieval churches in the country, this largely fourteenth century building with its distinctive octagonal tower is at least worth a look. Nantwich is also home to a number of the finest surviving Elizabethan houses – very much the genuine article rather than the results of Victorian restoration. They owe their existence to a fire that in 1583 largely destroyed the town and moved Queen Elizabeth to grant the town £2000 and rights to timber from Delamere, in order to rebuild.

Visit the Tourist Information Office (heavily signposted), arm yourself with the appropriate leaflets and explore!

39. Northwich and Great Budworth

Distance: 20.6 miles/32.5km.

Route: Northwich Railway Station – Marston – Great Budworth – Budworth Heath – Antrobus – Frandley – Comberbach – Weaverham – Hartford – Northwich Railway Station.

Surface: Tarmac.

Start: Greenbank station, Northwich (SJ645728).

Map: O.S. 118 (the Potteries).

Notes: The A49(T) into Weaverham is now the B5144 and the new A49(T) Warrington to Shrewsbury road is diverted away from Weaverham.

The Route

This route heads north away from Northwich. Along the initial stages of the ride various stretches of water will be passed, including Newman's Flash and Wincham Brook. From Great Budworth to Comberbach the route rolls along quiet country lanes in idyllic Cheshire countryside.

Finally the ride curves back towards Northwich passing through Weaverham and Hartford before arriving back at Northwich railway station.

Refreshment stops include: the Salt Barge, Marston; Little Chef, Dones Green A533/A49 crossroads; the Horns Inn and The Leigh Arms, Weaverham; the Green Bank pub and several stops in Northwich.

The Journey

Section a-b

Leave the station car park and ride towards the mini roundabout. On reaching the road junction, turn right. Follow the road ahead with Tesco now on the right. Continue to the end of what is the Manchester Road and give way at the junction of the A559. Turn left onto the A559 and

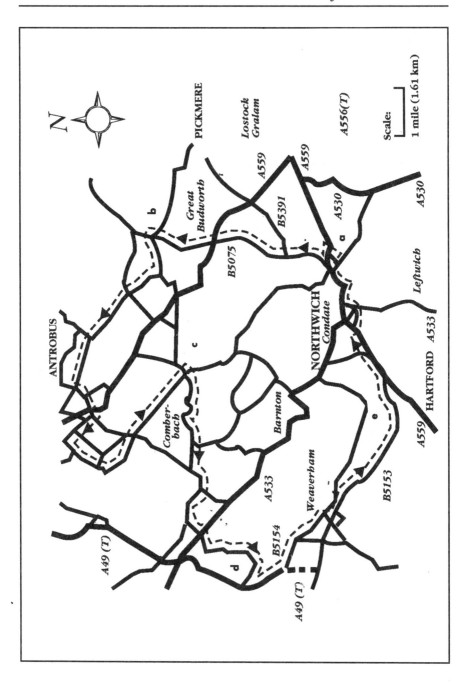

follow the road along until reaching the roundabout. At the roundabout, take the fourth exit onto the New Warrington road (B5075) to Wincham and Marston which are both three-quarters of a mile away at this point.

Follow the road ahead under the pylons and onwards towards Marston. Newman's Flash is on the left as the route travels into Marston. Ride through Marston over the hump-backed bridge which lies across the Trent and Mersey Canal and follow the road ahead.

Approximately 50 metres before reaching the main junction of the A559 turn right and ride the few metres to the second junction. Ride across the A559 onto Dark Lane which is signposted for Budworth. Ride down Dark Lane and up the other side into Great Budworth.

Section b-c

Continue along what is now Hield Lane until entering Great Budworth. At the junction turn left onto Park Lane, signposted for Knutsford. A few hundred metres along Park Lane, take the first left onto Westage Lane. Follow this towards the centre of Great Budworth.

On entering Great Budworth, take the first road on the right towards Antrobus and Warrington. Ride along the unmarked lane under the pylons and onward to Budworth Heath. Go to the end of what is now Heath Lane and ride across Belmont Road onto the Knutsford road, following the signs for Antrobus and Warrington at all times.

Ride along the Knutsford road to Antrobus post office and general store, in the centre of the village and on the right. Opposite the post office is School Lane. Turn left into this lane and continue straight ahead.

Ride along School Lane until the A559. Follow the road ahead for a few hundred metres and then take the first right off the A559 towards Frandley. In the centre of Frandley, turn right at the junction and ride towards Warrington along Well Lane. At the end of Well Lane turn left onto Old Mill Lane. Follow Old Mill Lane ahead, past Old Mill Farm on the right, Lester House Farm on the left and down what is now Goose Brook Lane. At the end of this lane turn left onto Hall Lane and a few metres after entering Hall Lane turn right onto Senna Lane.

Follow this lane, under the pylons and onwards into Comberbach. In the centre of Comberbach, turn right into Cogshall Lane which is opposite Comberbach Methodist Church.

Section c-d

Ride away from Comberbach along Cogshall Lane and under the pylons once again. Follow the route ahead. Cogshall Lane becomes Ash House Lane and runs past a Baptist Chapel on the left. Follow the lane ahead until the A533. Ride across the A533 onto Smithy Lane. Follow this until reaching Willow Green Lane – the first turning on the left.

Continue along Willow Green Lane, down over the Trent and Mersey Canal and down the hill towards the A49(T).

Section d-e

Turn left onto the A49; ride over the pavement section of the large black and white bridge and continue along the A49. Ride for approximately a quarter of a mile and take the first left for Weaverham on the B5144.

Follow the road ahead past the Mobil Service Station on the left and head up the hill. Take the first left into Well Lane and continue along the edge of Weaverham. At the end of Well Lane, turn right into Church Street. At the end of Church Street turn left by the Total petrol station onto the B5153. Follow the route ahead into Hartford.

Section e-a

After a brief encounter with Hartford, continue along the B5153 until it merges with the A559. Take the A559 towards Northwich. Ride through a set of traffic lights, go under a railway bridge and through an area of shops. Continue along the A559, down the hill past the Holy Trinity Church on the right. Nearing the bottom of the hill, take a right where the signs indicate Manchester on the (A56), Middlewich and Winsford consecutively. The road is called Chesterway.

Ride across the black and white bridge over the Weaver Navigation. Follow Chesterway, through the traffic lights, around the bend and over the River Dane until reaching a second set of traffic lights at Watling Street.

At this point, turn right onto the A559 once again. Follow the A559 back to the roundabout and take the fourth exit onto Station Road (B5082). At the end of Station Road, turn left at the traffic lights onto the Manchester road and finally take a right turn back to the station.

40. Northwich and Delamere Forest

Distance: 22 miles/35km

Route: Greenbank Station, Northwich – Leftwich – Davenham – Moulton – Whitegate – Little Budworth -Cotebrook – Delamere – Delamere Forest – Norley – Ruloe – Bryn – Northwich

Surface: Tarmac/Bridlepath

Start: Greenbank Station, Northwich (SJ645728)

Map: O.S. 117 (Chester) and O.S. 118 (the Potteries)

The Route

This circular route takes as its start one of Cheshire's three original 'wiches' or salt towns, Northwich, and heads out west to the ancient forest of Delamere. Although this suggests that along the route sites of historical interest will be encountered in abundance, this is not in fact the case. Northwich has been a victim of its own fortune – much of its heritage has been lost to subsidence, although a detour into the town centre will reward the cyclist with some almost picture-book architecture. This is the result of the townspeople of nineteenth century Northwich resorting to timber construction as the only form of building resilient to subsidence because they could simply be jacked back up to street level. In turn, Delamere is no longer the venerable royal forest it once was, but an overtly tourist friendly Forestry Commission plantation.

Nevertheless, this is still a most amiable route which, if taken at a leisurely pace, could comfortably take up an afternoon. Passing through a number of pretty villages (and thus past their pubs), by a museum which details the history of salt mining – an integral part of Cheshire's history, across the River Weaver, through Delamere Forest itself and past innumerable picnic sites (both official and unofficial) this easy ride is a delight.

The Journey

Section a-b

Turning right out of the station, head down the hill along the A559 towards the centre of town. Immediately after passing the tall spired church on your right, carefully turn off this road and then, via an impressive bridge, cross the River Weaver – noting as you do so the novel 'Flotel' away to your left. At the traffic lights you soon reach turn right to head for Leftwich. As you pass under the Manchester-Chester line you can see off to the right the Northwich Salt Museum. Housed in Weaver Hall, a nineteenth century workhouse, it explains the history of salt mining and therefore Northwich itself. Well worth a look.

Carrying on along the A533 through Leftwich, past Quincey's – a restaurant boasting deep fried ice-cream as a speciality and across the A556(T) by-pass, you'll eventually need to turn off right into Jack Lane, or the B5336. This will bring you to Moulton – as Jack Lane bends round to the left you should turn off right. Follow this lane past the Post Office and the Lion Hotel until it appears you have reached a dead end, albeit one with a view of the Weaver as it passes through the Vale Royal cut. Off to your left following the line of the fields is a bridlepath which you should now follow,perhaps needing to get off and wheel your bike for a spell. Being careful not to turn off right too soon and finding yourself in a farm, take the second turn to the right and head off down the hill and under the railway. Then, via a picturesque bridge, cross over the Weaver itself and cycle back up to the domain of the Department of Transport.

Turning right onto the lane, you immediately cross a narrow black and white bridge and then bear round to the left. This takes you past Bradford Mill, which has its water-wheel still intact and on view. Having dropped down into the pretty village of Whitegate, with its church shrouded behind tall conifers, you should turn left and cycle past the Post Office in Foxwist Green and, on reaching a crossroads, continue straight across. Having crossed a bridge over a dismantled railway, a sharp left turn will take you down to a picnic site and toilets set on what is now known as the Whitegate Way – a cinder path for walkers and horse riders along the old railway line.

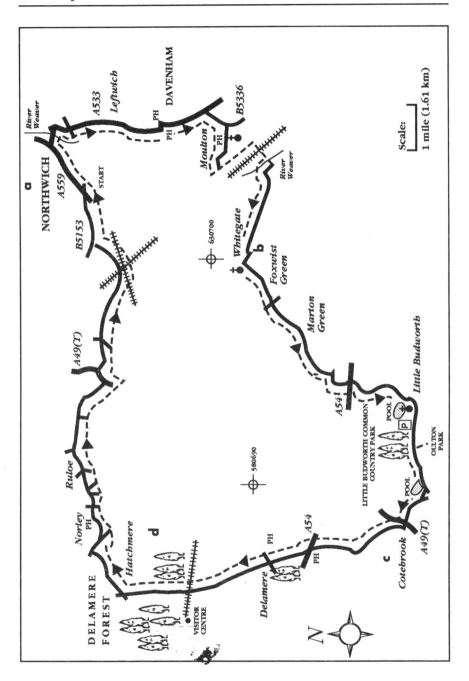

Section b-c

Returning to the lane, continue on across the A54 and then bear left into Mill Lane, past Budworth Pool and then through Little Budworth, with its red sandstone church and village pub, itself. Keep to the same lane as you pass on your right first the Egerton Arms and then a potential picnic-stop in the enchanting setting of an oak wood – Little Budworth Country Park. Then off to your left you pass the motor racing circuit of Oulton Park. After passing between a pool and its attendant derelict mill and restaurant you should turn right. Bearing right, you'll find yourself in Cotebrook, notable only for its Coffee Shop, where you should cross the A49(T) into Utkinton Lane, past the church, and then immediately right onto the B5152.

Section c-d

Follow this road across the A54 and then the A556(T), each junction being marked by pleasant pubs – the Fish Pool Inn and the ivy-clad Vale Royal Abbey Arms respectively. Heavily signposted on the left is the official Delamere Forest visitor centre, picnic site, cafe, car park and train station. From here it is possible to explore by foot the waymarked forest trails if a break from the saddle appeals. Returning to the B- road, however, as you carry on over the railway bridge you find yourself in the midst of the forest itself with numerous opportunities to stop. Although Delamere is an ancient forest, the deciduous trees that line the road are merely tokenism on the part of the Forestry Commission – modern Delamere is decidedly coniferous but nevertheless has its charm.

Section d-a

As you emerge from the trees and reach Hatchmere and the Delamere Forest Inn, you should turn right, bear right and then turn right at the T-junction into School Lane. This brings you into Norley and you should fork left just before the Methodist Chapel. Bearing left at the next junction, you pass the Tiger's Head (which is actually above one of the fireplaces) and follow the lane for two miles until you come to a junction with the A49(T) in the shadow of the Eden Valley dairy. Turn left and then immediately right down Millington Lane. Passing the Oaklands Pub and cycling over a spaghetti junction of railway line and country lane, you'll eventually reach the B5153 whereupon you should bear right to head back to Greenbank Station to finish your ride.

41. Poynton and Lyme Park

Distance: 13miles/21km.

Route: Poynton Station – Poynton village – Wood Lanes – Middlewood Way – Lyme Park – Disley – High Lane – Hockley – Poynton.

Surface: Tarmac, gravel.

Start: Poynton Station (SJ912837)/Middlewood Station (SJ945848)

Map: O.S. Landranger 109 (Manchester and surrounding area).

The Route

This ride can be started from one of two railway stations, each on separate lines, making it especially convenient. It takes in Lyme Park and Hall, and a considerable section of the Middlewood Way, a re-claimed railway line now used as a bridleway (for both cyclists and horseriders) and footpath.

The Journey

Section a-b

Start in Poynton, at the railway station, and turn left on the A5149 towards the centre, over the railway bridge. Continue to the traffic lights at the church and cross the main A523 road into Park Lane. Turn right into Bulkeley Road, just past the Farmers Arms pub, and turn left into Dickens Lane. Carry on for about $^2/_3$ mile, passing a large sports field on your left. The road bends sharply to the right, becoming the interestingly-named Moggy Lane. Continue to the T-junction with Wood Lane, then turn left into Wood Lane West and follow it as it meanders its way into the hamlet of Wood Lane, about half a mile along. Here, you'll find the Miners Arms, and a café opposite.

Section b-c

There's a real oddity, situated right on our route: at a right-hand corner in the middle of Wood Lanes, leave the road, and continue straight on,

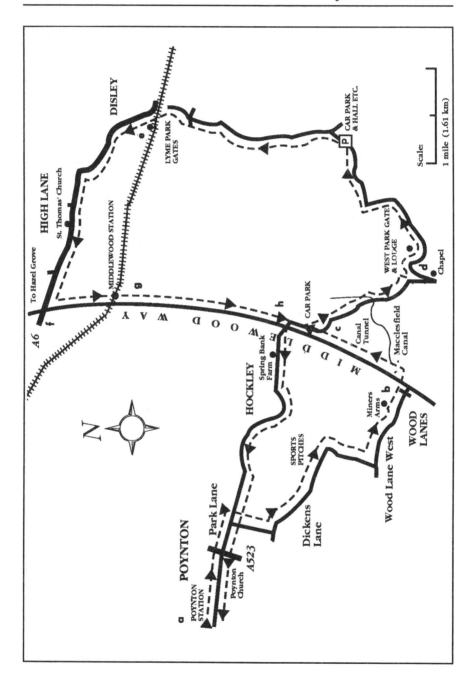

into a marked Private Road. Immediately you will see a fully-working Coca-Cola vending machine standing alone, by the side of the road! (anyone is welcome to use it.)

Just opposite this machine, signposts mark our joining point with the Middlewood Way, which is under a bridge. Follow the stepped path down onto the Way, and turn right (north) for about a mile. About halfway along this stretch, the Way seems to split, but it is actually just a parallel bridleway and footpath. Stay on the left of the 'split', to stay on the bridleway, and continue until you spot a car park on your right.

Section c-d

From the car park, turn right into the road, almost doubling back on the direction you have just travelled. Follow the road round a sharp left bend and continue along it as it takes you right out into the countryside. Eventually, you pas under the canal, through a narrow tunnel. Take extra care here, as it is very narrow, only one vehicle being able to pass at a time.

Continue along this road and pedal up the next hill. (Should this prove too strenuous, perhaps for children, there is a footpath which leaves the road just after the sharp right bend. This re-joins the main route at the Private Road, below.) Towards the top of this steep hill, there is a small chapel. Take a very sharp left here, to join a private road and head down to a bridge.

Section d-e

Cross the bridge, and then turn right, to see the West Gate of Lyme Park, just in front of a stone-built house. Go through the cyclists gate, *noting the sign instructing you to keep to the path.* Follow the path to the Hall; from the top of the hill, it's an exhilarating descent. At the car park, there's a coffee shop serving a range of snacks and drinks. Attractions at the park include a Nature Trail, the lake, the Hall itself and a pitch and putt course. Back on the route, take the main vehicle exit from the car park; follow the exit road over the railway bridge, which is quite narrow, and shortly emerge *carefully* onto the A6.

Section e-f

The route is simple now, for you simply follow the A6 into High Lane, enjoying more downward slopes, but the A6 *is* a busy major road. The road bends to the left and you suddenly find yourself amongst a proliferation of pubs. Pass or call at the Red Lion Inn, the Dog & Partridge, the Bulls Head and the Horse Shoe and you are soon back at the Middlewood Way.

Section f-g

Go down via a path, back onto the Way, and turn left (south-bound). About half a mile along, you again cross the railway line that you first met at the bottom of Lyme Park drive. Here is the second possible starting point for the ride, at Middlewood Station, on the Manchester – Macclesfield line.

Section g-h

From Middlewood Station, join the Middlewood Way on the bridge linking the two station platforms. Continue south for about another mile or so, going under Pool House Road, Prince Road and Barlow House bridges, all clearly marked with signs and distances to Macclesfield and Marple, in kilometres. Our 'junction' is Shrigley Road bridge, which is actually quite a difficult exit with a cycle. Alternatively, go to the next exit at Poynton Coppice Car Park.

Here you may get a sense of *déja vu*, for this is the point at which we left the Way previously. Again, we seem to double back on our route immediately: you leave the Way, turn left into the road, and simply follow this until you again meet Shrigley Road bridge (the first you'll come to). This is a most attractive detour, and worth doing.

Section h-a

Once over the bridge, head back towards Poynton. Pass Spring Bank Farm on your right, and simply follow this road as it heads back towards Poynton.

On the way, we go through the little village of Hockley, and eventually find ourselves back on Park Lane and back to Poynton station (if you joined the route at Middlewood Station, you need to turn left off Park Lane, into Bulkeley Road, just in front of the Farmers Arms pub. Then simply pick up the directions from there.)

42. Prestbury to Adlington

Distance: 15 miles/23km.

Route: Prestbury Railway Station – Hare Hill – Mottram St Andrew – Adlington Railway Station – Clark Green – Whiteley Green – Prestbury Railway Station.

Surface: Tarmac.

Start: Prestbury Railway Station (SJ904774).

Map: O.S. Landranger 109 (Manchester and surrounding area) and O.S. 118 (the Potteries).

The Route

This route does not use bridleways, but the roads and lanes are relatively quiet in this area. The ride might be unsuitable for small children as there are steep hills and narrow lanes. There are four pubs on the route of which two are on Prestbury's main street, plus a well-stocked village shop.

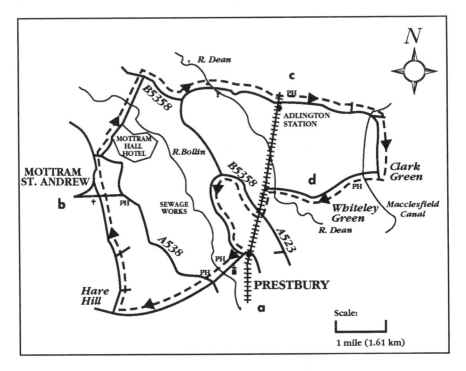

There are two places of interest *en route*:

– **Hare Hill** – this property belongs to the National Trust although Hare Hill House is privately owned. Hare Hill gardens are exquisite, especially in the spring time when the rhododendrons are at their best.

– **Adlington Hall** – the scene of Craft Fairs, Classical Concerts and other events. Visit the Hall and Gardens (check opening times) as a pleasant interlude in your cycle ride.

The start and finish point is at Prestbury Railway Station. The route passes Adlington Railway Station which could also be an ideal start point.

The Journey

Section a-b

Leave Prestbury Railway Station and turn left. Follow the road down, past the Admiral Rodney Pub and the village shop, both on the right. Go over the River Bollin and continue through Prestbury Village (past the Legh Arms/Black Boy – a pub with two names), to a small roundabout.

Take the road on your right past Royle's Garage and continue up to Chelford Road. Turn left here and cycle up the hill for around two miles until you reach Oak Road. If you want to take a break here and have a look around the gardens at Hare Hill continue up Chelford Road until you reach the entrance on your right, from here follow the signs to the gardens. To continue the route head down Oak Road which is on the right if you have just come from Prestbury and follow this for a further two miles.

Section b-c

At the end of Oak Road you reach Mottram St Andrew. Turn right here and immediately left down Moss Lane. Follow this road up to the junction, where you turn right and follow the road to the bottom. Soon you reach the A538, where you turn right. Take your next left turn – Mill Lane – going round the back of Mottram Hall Hotel, (on your right). You soon go over the River Bollin and then up to a crossroads.

Turn right here onto Wilmslow Road (B5358) and take a left fork down another Mill Lane. Follow this road over the River Dean and pass Adlington Hall on your right. You soon reach another set of crossroads, with the Legh Arms Pub directly opposite. Cross over the road (A523) onto Brookledge Lane and pass Adlington Railway Station on your right.

Section c-d

Follow Brookledge Lane, cycle past Adlington Primary School and go over the Middlewood Way (this is a disused railway line now used as a footpath and cycle-way). After crossing the Macclesfield Canal, take the next right down Sugar Lane and cycle for about a mile until you reach Holehouse Lane.

Turn right here and continue over the canal and Middlewood Way once again. Go downhill past the Windmill Pub on your left.

Section d-a

Follow Holehouse Lane over the River Dean before you reach the A523. Turn left here onto the main road and turn right onto Bovis Hall Lane. Go under the railway bridge and then take the next left down Butley Lanes. This leads to a T-junction opposite Prestbury Railway Station once again, but only after a nose-holding journey (depending on the wind direction) past the sewage works on the right.

43. Sandbach

Distance: 12 miles/19.5km.

Route: Scotch Common – Malkin's Bank – Hassall Green
– Hassall – Wheelock Heath – Railway Farm – Crabmill Farm – Moston Manor – Motor Works – Sandbach Station – Scotch Common.

Surface: Tarmac.

Start: Scotch Common Car Park (759609) or alternatively Sandbach station for those bringing their bikes by train (738615).

Map: O.S. 118 (the Potteries).

The Route

This route starts and finishes in the old market town of Sandbach which was granted its Royal Charter in 1565. This is celebrated with the 'Elizabethan Market' each year on May Day. A regular market is held every Thursday when stallholders and shoppers come from all over Cheshire and the Potteries.

Just after the start of the route you will pass the ancient Crosses in the old market square which are thought to have existed since the 7th century AD. The many pubs situated around the square will spoil you for choice and make an ideal place for refreshments either before or after your ride.

Country lanes provide the way to the quiet hamlet of Hassall Green by
the locks on the Trent and Mersey Canal. You will go past many farms
along quiet lanes to the main Crewe – Manchester railway line, going
through Moston Green and back to Sandbach via the station which is
confusingly situated in Elworth, 1.5 miles west of Sandbach on the A533.

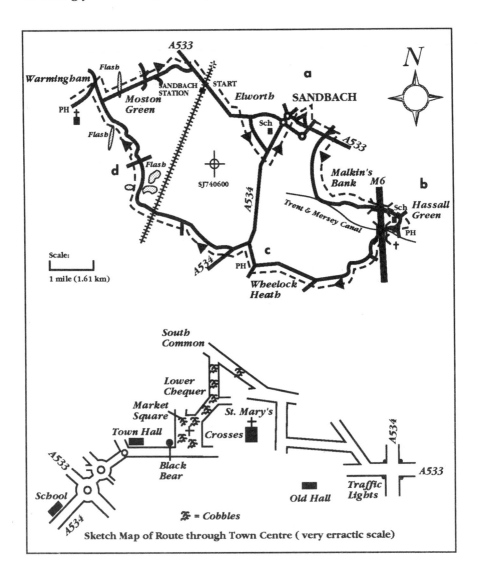

Sketch Map of Route through Town Centre (very erractic scale)

The Journey

Section a-b

If you are starting from Scotch Common Car Park, exit left onto the main road and turn left onto the A533 at the mini-roundabout by the Town Hall. Cycle down the hill out of the centre past the old market square and the church on the left, going as far as the traffic lights at the crossroads with the A534.

or

For those starting at the Station, turn left out of the station car park to the T-junction with the A533. Turn right here and follow the main road for just over a mile to a roundabout. Turn left towards the town centre and 100 yards further on, take the second exit at the next roundabout. The Town Hall will be facing you as you approach the mini – roundabout after another 100 yards. Turn right here along the A533 and cycle out of the centre to the traffic lights at the crossroads with the A534.

Go straight across at the crossroads and continue up the hill past the Almshouses on your left as far as the Sandpiper Public House on your left. Just after the pub, turn right along the road signposted to Malkin's Bank. Take care to avoid the parked cars on either side of the road continue out of Sandbach for 1 mile. Continue along this road, crossing over the motorway bridge, as far as the T-junction. Turn right here following the sign to Wheelock.

Entering Hassall Green, continue as far as the Romping Donkey pub just off the road on the left, where you can sit outside and enjoy a drink. After the pub, continue on the same road as before to the canal locks and the post office 200 yards further on.

Section b-c

Leaving the canal-side area, go over the bridge and down the slight hill round to the right, noting the strange pink, corrugated iron chapel. From here go under the motorway bridge, past the Hassall 'village' sign. Hassall itself consists of little more than a few farmhouses. Continue over the hill where the road bends to the right and then to the left. A sharp right-hand bend then follows with white railings on the inside.

Pass the farm tracks on your left and continue past the junction on the left along a long straight stretch, noting the farmhouse on the right, home to the Lockheath Herd of Friesians. Follow the road to the junction with what was previously the busy main Crewe Road at Wheelock Heath. This is now a quiet road linking the villages of Winterley and Haslington. Opposite the junction is the Holly Bush Public House (Greenall Whitley) with its restaurant, children's play area and beer garden.

Section c-d

Turn right at the junction in the direction of Sandbach and, after 200 yards, turn left into Elton lane. The road is now closed to cars a little further on to make way for the new by-pass (only indicated on the latest OS maps). Continue along Elton Lane past the permanent caravan park on the right. After a quarter of a mile, the road ends for cars. Bear right here where a small gate provides access only for cyclists and walkers onto the busy A534 by-pass. Directly opposite is a lane leading off the main road. It is advisable to dismount when crossing here.

Continue along the lane opposite, which although not too wide is almost free of vehicles. About a mile further on, turn right at the junction situated on a right-angled bend, following the sign to Warmingham. Pass the signs indicating road subsidence and continue under the railway bridge. Here, the road bears round to the right and continues up a slight hill. On either side, the small lakes (known as Flashes in the local area) are home to various forms of wildlife. Over on the right are the concrete pipes channelling the River Wheelock under the railway. Continue on for about a third of a mile until you reach the crossroads with Hall Lane.

Section d-a

Go straight across here and follow the lane where, at the time of writing, a new gas pipeline was being laid. The road bears round to the right at Crabmill Farm. Pass the attractive Limerick Hill Cottage and go down the small dip and back up past Croft Cottage, where many animals are to be found grazing in the smallholding. After a third of a mile, turn right by the house on your right. Continue towards Moston Green going down a steep dip with 'Flashes' on either side.

At the end of this lane, with Moston Manor slightly hidden by trees on the right, turn right. The road here runs through the small hamlet of Moston Green. After about half a mile, the road bends to the left towards Elworth. After a few hundred yards the roofs of the Foden motorworks come into view. Continue along the lane and over the canal, taking care on the narrow bridge.

The road bends to the left and then right up a slight hill into Elworth.

At the junction with the busy A533, turn right and continue into Sandbach. For those who have brought their cycles on the train, the station is situated about 200 yards on the right along the main road. If continuing into Sandbach, turn left to the town centre one mile further on at the roundabout. After 100 yards take the second exit at the next roundabout. The Town Hall will be facing you as you approach the mini-roundabout after 100 yards. Turn left here and Scotch Common car park is on your right 100 yards further on.

44. Styal, Moss Nook & Manchester Airport

Distance: 12 miles/20km.

Route: Styal Station – Kingsway – Handforth – Heald Green Station – Moss Nook – Manchester Airport & Cycle Track – Styal.

Surface: Tarmac, track.

Start: Styal Station/Heald Green Station (Parking available at both).

Map: O.S. Landranger 109 (Manchester and surrounding area).

The Route

This quite strenuous route has a very useful advantage, in that one can start it from either Styal or Heald Green Rail Stations. Essentially a road-based route, it takes in much of the suburban South Manchester and North Cheshire border. It also passes Manchester Airport affording some excellent views of incoming and outgoing aircraft. Part of it uses a purpose-built cycle track, running alongside some busy roads, obviously advantageous to anyone cycling with children, though it is necessary to cross the busy A538.

NOTE: crossing the A538 is extremely hazardous – please take extra care on this dangerous road. Likewise, heed our advice and do not attempt to cycle around busy roundabouts. It is unsuitable for inexperienced cyclists.

The Journey

Section a-b

From Styal Station, turn left, and continue down this fairly quiet road for some distance. You soon come to the Southfield Manor Nursing Home, at which point you leave the main road. Effectively, you continue straight on, down an unsurfaced road.

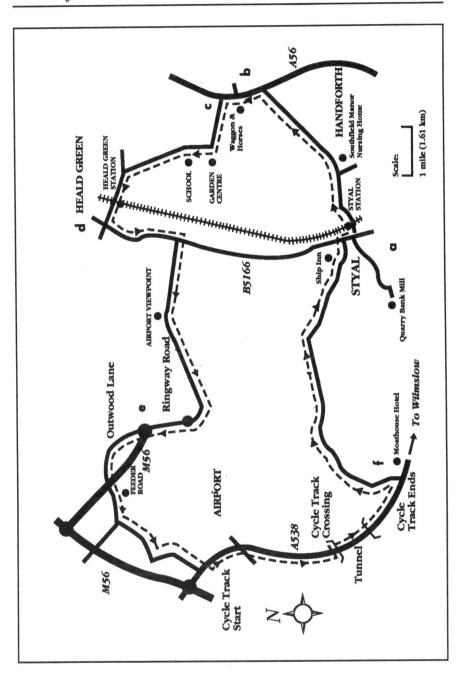

The 'road' soon comes to a conclusion, forking to two possible routes, both with metal gates and no-entry signs visible along them. Our route is the bridleway: the left-hand of the two. Ignore the no-entry signs – this applies only to vehicles – as there is an easily negotiable stile to the side of the gate. (This is not easily visible until you are some way down the lane.)

Follow the bridleway along its path, until it emerges onto an unsurfaced road, with a row of bungalows on the right. This gradually bends round to the right, and becomes well-surfaced. Carry on along it, until you emerge onto the A34 at its conclusion. Here, turn left, almost immediately arriving at the Waggon & Horses.

Section b-c

This serves food as well as drink, and could make for a most welcome point for a break! Once refreshed, (if you chose to stop) continue straight along the A34 at its junction, past the garage, and then prepare to take the first left, into Bolshaw Road.

Section c-d

Almost immediately, we are back in a rural atmosphere, down this attractive, tree-lined road.

Follow Bolshaw Road almost to its end, (where there is a Garden Centre), but turn right into Cross Road just before this. Pass Bolshaw Primary School, and carry along this road to its conclusion, where you turn left into bustling Finney Lane.

We are now in the centre of Heald Green, soon to find ourselves at the station which can serve as an ideal stopping point, being safely off the road.

Section d-e

At the station that you may catch your first of many spectacular views of aircraft near the airport.

From Heald Green Station, turn left and continue until you meet the junction with the B5166, where you again turn left. Take care here, especially if you are with children, for this is quite a busy junction. Follow this road for about half a mile, and right into Ringway Road, a much quieter road. (It may actually be easier to dismount and cross the road by foot here).

Pass Primrose Cottage Nursery on your left, very shortly afterwards coming to an excellent viewing area for "plane spotting" at Shadowmoss Road (you will probably not be alone here!).

When you resume your journey, get back onto Ringway Road, and continue along it, right onto the main airport roundabout. It is *very advisable to dismount* just before here, as this is a motorway feeder roundabout, and therefore not the most cyclist-friendly environment.

Section e-f

Take the final exit from this roundabout, clearly marked as Outwood Lane. Initially, this twists and turns, but soon becomes a much quieter country road, which you follow round past Etrop Grange Hotel, and over the motorway feeder road bridge.

Immediately after this, you can join a cycle track that will take you right up to the M56 junction with the A538. Stay on the cycle track, taking the first left turning. The track then crosses to the right hand side of the road (TAKE EXTRA CARE) and continues for about two-thirds of a mile, where it crosses to the left-hand side; you then go through the long airport tunnel, beneath the runway. You might be in for a surprise here – turn the page and take a look!

After the tunnel, the cycle track ends, and we join the main road for just a few yards, until we turn left down a minor road, following the sign for Styal.

Section f-a

The second hard climb begins here, and it may well be necessary to dismount, particularly as this stretch is sometimes congested with parked cars. Follow this road, twisting and turning for about two miles, when we arrive back in Styal. Notice the distinctive airport radar tower along this stretch.

Coming back into Styal, welcome refreshment can be found at the Ship Inn. Directions to historic Quarry Bank Mill are also clearly marked around here.

Just past the Ship Inn, the end of this road brings a right turn onto the B5166. Almost immediately, we turn left again, into Station Road and back to the station car park, where we finish.

A sight to stop you in your tracks on the cycleway alongside the A538
(by permission of Manchester International Airport plc; photograph by Crocodile)

45. Tattenhall and Malpas

Distance: 36 miles/58km.

Route: Tattenhall – Clutton – Lower Carden – Stretton – Shocklach – Horton Green – Malpas – Hampton Heath – Harthill – Burwardsley – Tattenhall

Surface: Tarmac

Start: The Letters Inn, Tattenhall (SJ487585)

Map: O.S. 117 (Chester).

The Route:

This circular route stretches from the Peckforton Hills across the western half of the Cheshire plain to the Welsh border, and is probably, if done in its entirety, among the hardest rides in this book. For a county that is mostly plain this doesn't, of course, say much but this route involves climbing the 'mid' Cheshire ridge twice – certainly rewarding but perhaps a challenge to those seeking comfortable Sunday afternoon wanderings.

If you're not yet put off, this ride's charm lies in the countryside in which it is set – very much unspoilt by dint of its isolation: you could never mistake this for commuter belt Cheshire! The stunning views afforded by climbing the hills are worth the entire days cycling alone, but this ride also takes in the pretty market towns of Malpas and Tattenhall, a working mill at Stretton and Cheshire Candle Workshops, plus part of the route is stretched along a Roman road.

The ride should take about three to five hours, although this could be less if you take up one of the short cuts offered in the main route description and there's the usual variety of hostelries along the route to save you making those sandwiches! This corner of Cheshire being inaccessible by train, you could start wherever you wish but for our purposes we'll take as our starting point Tattenhall.

The Journey

Section a-b

Having found somewhere in Tattenhall to park, make your way to the Letters Inn *(sic)* in the centre of this charming town and then head off south along the main road to begin your route. Soon after, the road bends sharply round to the right and thereby out of the town you should turn off left and head up the slight hill which nevertheless

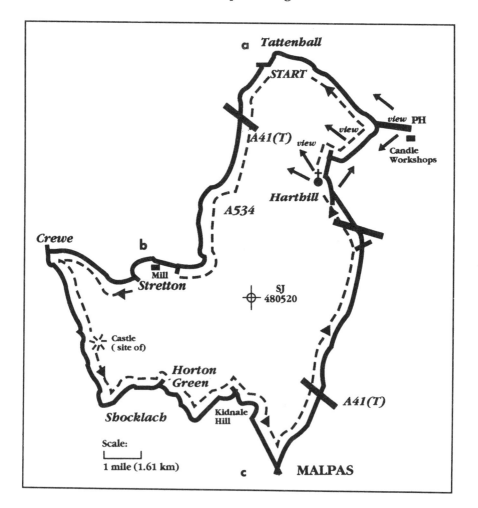

affords great views of the Peckforton Hills. Coming down the other side you then with care should cycle across the A41(T) and follow the lane you now find yourself on, perhaps being lucky enough to glimpse a herd of Longhorn Cattle. Well away to your left you'll be able to make out, lying in the shadow of the Mid-Cheshire ridge, Bolesworth Castle – actually a private residence of 18th/19th century construction. Visually impressive from this distance all the same.

When the road bends sharply round to the right, turn left into a very narrow lane which almost immediately brings you to the A59 which you cross to find yourself in a lane bordered by Carden Park Golf Course on one side and a tree covered incline on the other. Following this lane round to the right and then carrying straight on past the impressive gate-house entrance to the Golf Course as the lane sweeps away to the left to make your way up to the tourist friendly Stretton Mill which is well worth a stop.

Section b-c

On reaching the end of this lane, turn left and as soon as the opportunity presents itself, turn right onto what soon shows itself to be a lane along the line of a Roman green road, which would have led from Malpas to one of the Dee's ancient bridging points at Farndon. If nothing else this makes for easy, pleasant cycling – always a welcome characteristic! Two miles of this brings you to Crewe which, consisting as it does of a couple of farms and a handful of cottages, is considerably smaller than its east Cheshire namesake. Turn left such that the River Dee (i.e. the Welsh Border) is on your right and head south to Shocklach, passing as you do so the site of a Norman border castle, as marked on the map. Much of Shocklach's church dates back to the same era.

As soon as you enter the village, turn left past the Bull Inn and head up to the seventeenth century cottages of Horton Green. Here you turn right and head for Overton Scar by bearing left. This brings you to a junction with the Roman Road, a different stretch of which you passed along earlier, and you should turn right to make your way to Malpas. The modern road swerves violently around the hill that now lies in front of you but the Roman path over it can still be made out.

As you enter Malpas, a sharp turn to the left along the B5069 presents the route you take out of the town but you may wish to explore and rest a little. The name, French in origin, means 'bad pass' and you'll be unsurprised to learn that Malpas was once home to a Norman castle overlooking the borderlands. The market town's best surviving feature is undoubtedly the church of St Oswalds, although it has been remarked that the entire town is a microcosm of all that is best about Cheshire and easily justifies a break in your journey.

Section c-a

Heading back out of town, in a couple of miles you reach a roundabout overlooked by the New Inn, where you head straight across by taking the second exit. Follow this lane through all its twists and turns until the A534, having just passed Holy Trinity church. This marks the start of the first of the hard yet rewarding climbs. Crossing the A-road, follow the lane bearing right up to the hilltop village of Harthill, which besides the impressive church of All Saints also has one of Cheshire's most striking views. On a clear day you can easily see along the length of the Peckforton Hills to Beeston castle, across the Cheshire Plain and border to the Welsh hills and north to the industrial works of the Wirral.

Continuing on along the lane, head downhill – those already sick of ascents or who simply want to shorten the ride will find that this lane takes them all the way down on to the simple pleasures of the plain and on into Tattenhall. For those who want more, a right turn (signposted Candle Workshops) as you drop down the hill is the way forward.

Following this lane through all its climbs and satisfying drops again takes you to Tattenhall, but if you were to turn off as signposted to head for the Candle Workshops as you passed through Burwardsley (pronounced Boosly) a punishing climb will take you up to the Candle workshops and, perhaps more importantly, the attached Hayloft restaurant and the nearby (and highly recommended) Pheasant Inn with its gorgeous views over to the Welsh hills.

At the much-vaunted Candle workshops themselves you can see intricately designed candles in all stages of creation and perhaps attempt to have a go yourself. Inevitably, the finished product is very much on sale, together with a variety of crafts material. Its ample car-parking would make this a good start/finish point if you were willing to commit yourself at the start of the day to such a gruelling climb at the very end. The choice is yours.

To finish your ride, retrace your route as far back as Burwardsley (as opposed to Higher Burwardsley) and then turn right to cycle down to Tattenhall.

46. Warrington, Winwick and Culcheth

Distance: 12 miles/19km.

Route: Padgate Station – Houghton Green – Winwick – Croft – New End Lane – Kenyon – Culcheth – Little Town – Padgate Station.

Surface: Tarmac.

Start: Padgate Station (SJ631900).

Map: O.S. Landranger 109 (Manchester and surrounding area).

The Route

The ride starts at Padgate station on the edge of Warrington, which means there's less city traffic to deal with. From Padgate the route heads north. As the road takes you into the countryside the scene is of a very flat landscape which could easily be East Anglia rather than the usual gently rolling hills of Cheshire. After crossing two motorways, the route curves around southwards and heads back into Cheshire. Shortly after passing through the village of Little Town the ride leads back into Warrington and back to Padgate.

Plenty of refreshment stops are available, including the Millhouse, by the roundabout at Houghton Green village; the Horseshoe and the General Elliot at Croft; The Plough at New End Lane.

The Journey

Section a-b

If coming from central Warrington, as you arrive in Padgate station do the following: Leave the station car park, turn left and ride up the small hill to the junction. From the other side of the platform, ride up to meet the nearest road to the station.

Follow the signs for Leigh and the A574. Follow the road ahead until reaching a roundabout. Continue across the roundabout to the second exit leading to Blackbrook, a quarter of a mile away. Ride along Blackbrook Avenue and at the traffic lights cross the junction Insall Road and Hilden Road. Continue to a second roundabout; signposted at this point are the villages of Houghton Green, Winwick and Croft.

Ride straight on as before. At the third roundabout, take the second exit once again and pass the Millhouse pub on the left. Go along Millhouse Lane into Houghton Green village. Almost immediately after passing out of the village ride over the M62. Continue ahead into level countryside. The M6 motorway is seen to the right before turning into a sharp left-hand bend. Continue for a short distance until reaching the junction.

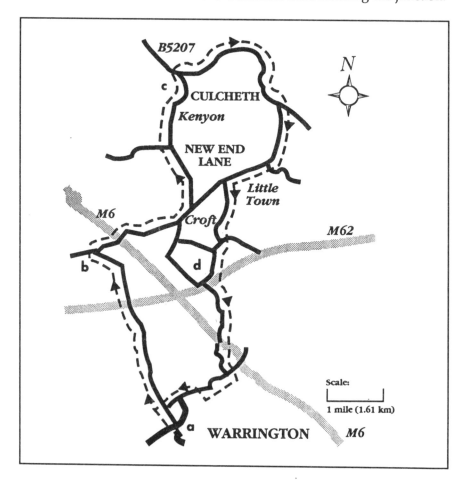

Section b-c

At the junction, turn right onto Myddleton Lane towards Croft and Culcheth. Follow the road ahead into Southwarth Lane. Bear left, go over the M6, follow the road around to the right and ride under the pylons. The road curves left and right for a short distance before entering a 30mph zone and Croft village. Ride through the village before taking the first major turning left by the General Elliot pub. The road is clearly signposted for Lowton which is $2^1/_2$ miles away.

Ride along Stone Pit Lane for about two miles until you reach the Plough pub on the right. Just after the pub, turn right into Kenyon Lane. Continue through a 30mph zone away from Stone Pit Lane and New End Lane village. Follow the road into the village of Kenyon. Pass the wooded area on the right and ride over the main Manchester-Liverpool railway. Immediately after, ride up to the junction with the B5207. Turn right here onto Witton Lane and ride on towards Culcheth.

Go over a dismantled railway before coming back into Cheshire a few hundred metres along the road. Ride over the Manchester-Liverpool railway line once again and enter Culcheth. Continue along Broseley Lane past Leigh Golf Club, then turn right just before Culcheth Methodist Church.

Section c-d

After the right turn, ride down Hob Hey Lane to a junction. Turn right into Wigshaw Lane, ride up the hill and back into Culcheth.

Follow the road out of Culcheth and continue down towards Little Town. Take the second left turn into Lady Lane and, after riding past Christ Church on the left, bear right. Turn right out of the junction onto Cross Lane then turn left into Spring Lane. Continue past the Croft Riding Centre on the right and, at the end of Spring Lane, turn left.

Section d-a

Just after turning left, ride under the M62 and up and over one of the motorway slip-roads. The road name changes from Mill House Lane to Locking Stumps Lane. You are now heading back into Warrington. Shortly after passing over the motorway, turn left by an office building. Ride along Crab Lane to a roundabout, and take the third exit off the roundabout along the A574 towards Padgate.

47. Wilmslow: Morley and Lindow

Distance: 9 miles/13km.

Route: Lindow Common – Paddock Hill – Lindow End – Noonsun Farm – Knolls Green – Graveyard Farm – Morley Green – Lindow Common.

Surface: Tarmac, gravel, cinder surfaces.

Start: Lindow Common car park (SJ833814).

Map: O.S. Landranger 109 (Manchester and surrounding area) and O.S. 118 (the Potteries).

The Route

This short ride uses a variety of quiet lanes and bridleways. The bridleways are often frequented by walkers, less so by horse riders, so take care and be considerate to other users. Because so few busy roads are used, and also because it is relatively short, even a family with young cyclists can easily complete the route inside a couple of hours. There are, also, no fewer than four pubs – so no one need go hungry or thirsty. But remember that it is an offence to be drunk in charge of a cycle – so restrain yourself.

The ride begins at the car park on Racecourse Road, off the A538 (Wilmslow to Altrincham Road), opposite the Boddington Arms. Parking is easy for those bringing their bikes by car and, if coming from Wilmslow station, just follow the signs to Altrincham – this will add about 1.5 miles to the journey. If you have time, take a walk around the common, designated as a Site of Special Scientific Interest.

The Journey

Section a-b

On leaving the Lindow Common car park, turn left along Racecourse Road and continue for a few hundred metres to the first road on your right – Newgate – which, at the time of writing, leads past the County Council waste disposal site.

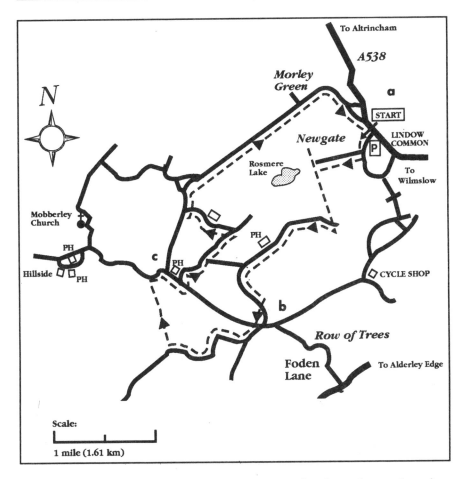

At the end of Newgate, you come to a crossroads where the road surface deteriorates. Turn left here along the track marked "Bridle Path to Moor Lane". You have to heave your cycle over obstructions at both ends of the track, designed to prevent motorcyclists from wreaking havoc.

At the far end of the bridle path, the track becomes a tarmac lane. As this exits onto a road turn right, with some shops facing you, and continue along this somewhat bumpy lane, past Ned Yates Garden Centre.

At a Y-junction, turn left along a rough track towards Barlow House Farm. This is another "road used as a public path" (RUPP); the landowners welcome careful cyclists, but not horses. They even put up warning notices when they've cut the hawthorn hedges – in case you get a puncture!

Cycle along this stony path, passing the farmhouse and superbly renovated tythe barn on your right. After exiting from the drive, you pass – or maybe call at – the Plough & Flail, where it is particularly pleasant to sit *al fresco* on a summer evening.

Shortly after the pub, fork left at a Y-junction – pausing to admire the pool on your right (Note the "Deep Water" warning). Turn left again down Paddock Hill Lane and continue to the cross-roads at the busy Knutsford Road.

Section b-c

Cross this road with care and then, after a short distance, turn right into the intriguingly – named Noah's Ark Lane. Continue for about a mile, passing a sewage farm in the dip on your left, and then coming to Noon Sun Farm at the very end of the lane.

Turn right here and right again into Faulkners Lane. This takes you past the Frozen Mop and leads back to the busy Knutsford Road again – here called Moss Lane, signifying the route to the once – massive Lindow Moss or perhaps one of the other peat extraction areas hereabouts. Turn right at the T-junction with this busy road, the B5086.

Section c-a

Cycle along the B5086 and either;

– turn left just before the Bird in Hand to lead back to Wilmslow; only do this if time is short, or

– go past the Bird in Hand and turn first left along Moss Lane (presumably, this way was once the continuation of the Moss Lane we've just cycled along, before the modern road was built).

The first option is easy; so, continuing with the alternative, cycle along Moss Lane and, shortly after the dwelling called "Anna Purna", turn left into a lane with a "No through Road" sign – but don't let this disconcert you.

Continue along this lane and pass Egerton's vehicle repair yard on your left; slow down now and look for a very narrow track on your left indicated by a footpath sign (except when it has been removed) and, at the time of writing, with a chicken run alongside it. Despite the sign, this is actually a bridleway and is well used by both cyclists and horse-riders.

The point of interest along here is the Quaker graveyard, which you come to after a couple of hundred metres, on the right-hand side, behind a low brick wall. This was one of the very earliest Quaker burial sites in England and was attached to a nearby Meeting House. The gravestones date back to 1659; some of the 19th century graves were protected from body-snatchers by alternate layers of soil and straw, through which it is difficult to dig! In 1831, the local Quakers moved to their new home on Altrincham Road.

The Quaker Graveyard

Leave the graveyard and continue along a widening track, at the end of which you turn right and head towards Morley Green. This road is a little busier than others on the route – take care after about a mile where the road dips down to Burleyhurst Bridge: the road has been widened, giving an opportunity for cars to be driven at alarming speeds along here.

After climbing up from Burleyhurst Bridge, pass through Morley Green and then, with Stratton's space-age showroom in sight, and after passing a group of houses on your right, turn right along a rough and stony track. This might be hard on your posterior, but it protects you from the perils of the A538!

Where this track reaches the main road, push your bike for the short stretch of pavement until you reach another track that runs behind the Boddington Arms and on to Racecourse Road. Turn left here and you're back to where you started.

48. Wilmslow and Great Warford

Distance: 12 or 15 miles/19km or 24km.

Route: Lindow Common – Morley Green – Mobberley – Great Warford – Row of Trees – Lindow Common.

Surface: Tarmac, hard-core, grass.

Start: Lindow Common car park (SJ833814).

Map: O.S. Landranger 109 (Manchester and surrounding area) and O.S. 118 (the Potteries).

The Route

Highlights to be seen include:

❏ The church tower climbed by Mallory (of Everest fame)

❏ Flamingoes and penguins, in the middle of a Cheshire village

The journey starts from Lindow Common car park (see comments in previous bike ride if starting from Wilmslow Town Centre) and goes through quiet lanes on the outskirts of Mobberley. One interesting bridleway is included and – for those with mountain bikes – there are two more "interesting" routes.

The ride is easily completed in a couple of hours or so but is perhaps best for those with some experience as the bridleway routes, though possible on a touring bike, might be difficult for young children. Some extra "Mountain Bike" routes are included for those who fancy them, but be warned – they are *really* muddy in the winter. There are a couple of stretches of moderately busy roads, though these are rarely used by heavy vehicles.

The Journey

Section a-b

Starting from Lindow Common car park, ride out to the Altrincham Road and turn left. After the Texaco Garage and the super-luxury car showroom, turn left again and head along this relatively quiet road, through Morley Green.

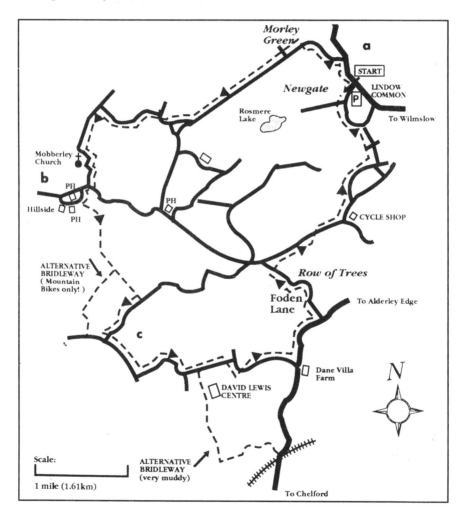

After a little over a mile and just after a succession of "road bends", "road narrows" and "Welcome to Mobberley" signs, fork right along a pleasant country lane. Then take the second turning left into Davenport Lane and notice some really attractive thatched and black and white houses and cottages. A far cry from suburbia!

Turn left at the end of Davenport Lane, signposted to Mobberley. Left again at the next T-junction and you'll come to Mobberley Church. It's 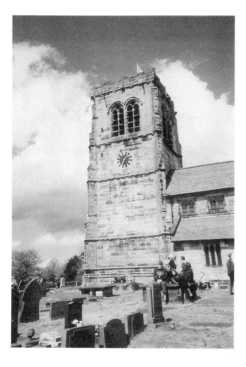 worth stopping here to go inside and inspect the stained glass window dedicated to Mallory, of Mallory and Irving fame, who attempted to climb Everest in 1924. Mallory is a popular name hereabouts, with several rectors having the same name. There are stocks outside the church, an excellent inn opposite and the cricket ground behind – the epitome of the English village!.

Continue along this lane to the main road. Turn right, then first left into Mill Lane. There are two pubs here – the Bull's Head and the Roebuck. If you have the time, visit the Hillside Ornamental Bird Centre just past the Roebuck. It is a remarkable place, with penguins, pelicans, flamingoes, kookaburras and lots more. You'll need a couple of hours (or more) to take it all in, and there's an excellent cafe for visitors.

Section b-c

Your route is along the very minor lane just before the Roebuck and almost opposite the Bull's Head. Cycle along this lane and it gets noticeably rougher. At the entrance to a field, turn right (at a bridleway sign) and cycle uphill. Go through a gate and follow the right-hand field boundary, with the hedge on your right. Go around the edge of the field (there is no track as such, and it could be muddy in the winter) until you reach a small pool and a gate in the top left-hand corner of the field.

Go through a gate and again cycle along the right-hand edge of the field (no track here either!) and head towards a large barn. You reach a gate, which you either go through or climb over. There is an intersection of bridleways – see map. Intrepid mountain bikers can turn right here, at first following a tarmac track, then forking right through a gate at a bridleway sign. The rest continue straight on, turning right at the T-junction. At the next T-junction, turn left, just before a right-hand bend, into Pinfold Lane. After a further kilometre, turn left again into Kell Green Lane.

Section c-a

At a T-junction, take yet another left turn towards the magnificent building housing the David Lewis Centre. Again, for mountain bikers only, there is a bridleway on the right after about 100m on the right-hand side. This runs along a good track initially but, like the other bridleway on this route, forks right through a gate and heads through a field (with no evidence of a track) through a wood. At the end of this, there is a left-turn taking you near to the traffic lights where the railway line crosses the Chelford road – see map.

The rest of us continue ahead, passing the Stag's Head. At the T-junction, turn right opposite to Dane Villa Farm. Continue for 1 Km along this fairly busy road, then turn left into Foden Lane. This runs past the back of Wilmslow Golf Course. At the T-junction, turn right and continue for about 1.5 Km, passing North Cheshire Garages. Take the next turn left to Wilmslow. noting Tom Royle's Cycle Shop at the junction – just in case.

You're back in suburbia now. Cycle along Knutsford Road, then turn left into Gravel Lane. Follow this road until a large green area at a junction and turn left up South Oak Lane. Cross carefully into Oak Lane (inconsiderate motorists park so as to obstruct your view at this **very dangerous crossroads**) and continue to Lindow Common car park.

Note – if you have not visited the Common, push your bike through the stile at the Oak Lane End and walk back to the car park alongside the lake. Cycling is not permitted but it's a worthwhile diversion.

49. Winsford and Church Minshull

Distance: 18 miles/29km.

Route: Winsford Station – Clive Green – Walleys Green – Cross Lane – Church Minshull – Paradise Green – Wettenhall – Stockerlane – School Green – Hebden Green – Littler – Schoolsways Green – Winsford Station.

Surface: Tarmac.

Start: Winsford Station (SJ671660).

Map: O.S. 118 (the Potteries).

The Route

The route leaves Winsford station and travels south, then heads along the A530 and west towards the small village of Church Minshull. From here, we wind our way around narrow country lanes, with views of the Frodsham Hills to the west and flat Cheshire pastureland all around.

On the outskirts of Winsford the route follows a bridleway from School Green to Hebden Green and then east back to Winsford station.

The Journey

Section a-b

Leave Winsford station, join the roundabout and take the third exit. Ride over the grey bricked bridge and onwards down the hill past the Brighton Belle pub on the left. On reaching the traffic lights turn right into Clive Lane.

Follow the road ahead parallel with the railway line, ride under the pylons and through Clive Green. A few hundred metres after Clive Green the road narrows to a single lane as it passes over the River Weaver. Take care at this point as oncoming traffic cannot be easily seen.

Continue along Clive Lane until the A530 is reached. At the junction turn right and follow the road ahead. Follow the A530 over the railway

line and ride past the Verdin Arms pub on the right. A few metres past
the pub on the left is a sign for Minshull Vernon.

Continue down the road until a red sandstone cross commemorating
Queen Victoria's reign can be seen at the head of a road junction on the
right. Turn right at this point and follow the sign for Church Minshull
which is two miles away.

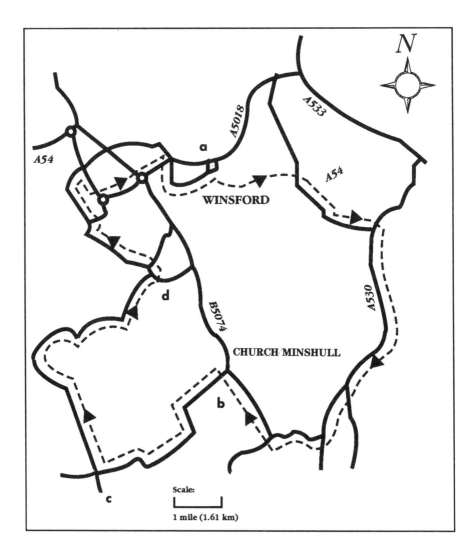

Section b-c

Ride along the route from the junction to the end of Cross Lane. At the end of the lane turn right and follow the signs for Church Minshull which is three-quarters of a mile away.

Follow the road ahead as you ride under the pylons again. Continue along the route, ride over the Shropshire Union anal and onwards to Church Minshull. Before entering Church Minshull, again ride over the River Weaver.

On arriving in Church Minshull, turn right at the junction onto the B5074 for Winsford which is four miles away.

Follow the B5074 out of Church Minshull and up the hill. Continue for a mile until you reach the Lea Green filling station on the right. A few hundred metres after the filling station, turn left down Paradise Lane.

Follow the lane ahead until you reach Paradise Farm. At this point the lane will take a very sharp left. Follow the lane round until you reach Paradise Green where the lane then takes a sharp right-hand bend.

On reaching the end of Paradise Lane turn right at the junction. Follow the road round to the left and continue along the road which heads west, with views of Delamere and the Frodsham hills.

Ride along what is now Minshull Lane until you arrive at the junction.

Section c-d

At the end of Minshull Lane turn right at the junction and follow the signs for Wettenhall which is three quarters of a mile away; Winsford which is now 5 miles away.

As you ride out of Wettenhall Green ride past the Little Man Inn on your left. Follow the road ahead towards Wettenhall. Continue along Winsford Road through Wettenhall past the Boot & Slipper pub and onwards out of Wettenhall. Ride down the hill, over Wettenhall Brook and up the other side along Winsford Road. Follow the road round as it curves back in the direction of Winsford.

Note: At Ash House on the OS map at SK622633 there is a discreetly hidden airfield called Bryan's Landing; worth a look, though this is not on the route.

Follow the road ahead, taking a sharp left past the gates of Wettenhall Hall. Ride through the village of Darnhall and down Winsford Road.

Section d-a

At the end of Hall Road you arrive in School Green. Turn left at the junction onto Darnhall School Lane. A few metres past the junction take the first left onto the bridleway.

The surface is gravel and very uneven with numerous pot holes. Ride past the white gate and onwards until a grey metal gate is reached. From here the track ceases and grass prevails. Follow the bridleway signs across the field to Hebden Green.

On reaching the rusting gate at Hebden Green, turn right down the lane and follow it left around to the farm. On reaching the farm take the left fork of the lane and ride down towards a white gate. Turn left at the gate onto a tarmac lane.

Ride over a drainage ditch and follow the lane ahead. At Lane End Farm, on the left-hand side of the lane, turn right and travel along a narrow bumpy track until reaching the A54.

Turn right onto the A54 and follow the signs for Winsford town centre. At the first roundabout, take the first exit and ride on down along the A54 until you reach the second roundabout. At this point take the second exit.

Winsford station is two miles away from here. Ride through the first set of traffic lights and down the hill until you reach a large angular-shaped roundabout. Take the third exit off this roundabout and follow the signs back to the station via the A54.

50. Winsford and Hartford

Distance: 15.5 miles/25km.

Route: Winsford Station – Wharton Green – Moulton – Mere Heath – Davenham – Hartford – Whitegate – Nova Scotia – Winsford Station.

Surface: Tarmac.

Start: Winsford Station (SJ671660).

Map: O.S. 118 (the Potteries).

The Route

The route takes you north from the centre of Winsford, briefly through its industrial estate, and towards the villages of Moulton and Davenham.

From here the route travels west towards Hartford which is twinned with Mornant in France. After passing through Hartford you travel south into the attractive Vale Royal district.

After passing through the villages of Whitegate and Foxwist Green, the route meanders around a number of quiet country lanes before eventually coming back to the outskirts of Winsford and back to the Station.

The Journey

Section a-b

After leaving Winsford Station, go around the roundabout and take the third exit. Ride over the grey bricked bridge and down the hill past the Brighton Belle Pub on your left and towards the traffic lights at the end of the hill. Turn left at the traffic lights and ride through Winsford Industrial Estate.

Pass 40mph signs and the Iveco warehouse on the left. After leaving the Industrial Estate, the road curves right and goes downhill. At the end of this road is a roundabout. Turn right here to Northwich on the A5018. A

few hundred metres along this road, turn left up Jack Lane, (the B5336)
to the village of Moulton.

Section b-c

After riding into Moulton the road takes a sharp curve to the right. On
the left is the Lion Pub (food and Tetley Bitter) and further down the
road is The Travellers Rest. Passing through the residential part of
Moulton, Jack Lane meets the A533. Turn left here and ride towards
Davenham.

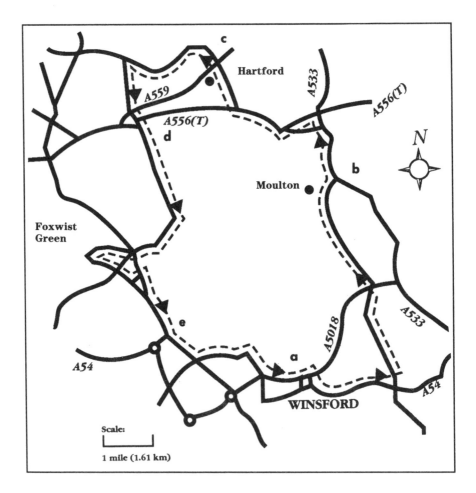

Riding down the hill into Davenham Town Centre, you pass several antique shops on the left and right of the road and follow the sharp bend left. On the left, there is the Old Fellow Arms. Follow the road ahead and over the zebra crossing.

Continue to the roundabout and turn left onto the A556(T) which has a cycle lane running parallel with the road. This goes west towards Hartford. After a quarter of a mile or so, the gravel cycle track ends and continues in the form of a tarmac slip road for the houses on the left. Ride down the hill towards the parallel pale blue bridges. Eventually the slip road ends and the gravel cycle track resumes.

Ride over the River Weaver and up the hill towards Hartford. On arriving at the signpost for Hartford and Weaverham, stop. It is advisable to dismount when crossing this busy dual carriageway.

Section c-d

After crossing the dual carriageway, ride past the sign denoting the twinning of Hartford with Mornant and follow the road straight ahead. Hartford is three-quarters of a mile from here.

After passing Hartford Hall Hotel on the right, continue along School Lane until you reach the sign for 'The Green'. Follow the road ahead which now bears left. At the end of the road, and on the right, is St John the Baptist Church and on the left is the Red Lion Pub. At this junction, turn right and take the A559 for Northwich. A few hundred metres down the A559, turn left at the traffic lights onto Bradburns Lane.

Ride along Bradburns Lane with the Grange School on the left. Ride over the railway line and, just after it, is a church with a spire. At the junction, turn left onto the B5153 and carry on until Hodge Lane, (on your left) signposted to Sandiway and Cuddington.

Ride down Hodge Lane and over a railway bridge. Another railway bridge. Another railway line runs parallel to the road at this point. A few hundred metres after the bridges, take the first left down Little Dales Lane (un-signposted); continue along the lane, under the pylons, and then under a railway bridge. Carry on up to the end of the lane and turn left to the junction of the A559. Turn right towards Winsford which is a little under five miles away. Ride over the bridge which crosses the A556(T).

Section d-e

On reaching Whitegate, St Mary's Church is on the right. Follow the road ahead and ride down the hill through Whitegate. The road then climbs a steep hill before reaching Foxwist Green.

Follow the road to a junction where you turn left into Dalefords Lane and follow the signs for Sandiway and Cuddington. A few hundred metres along Dalefords Lane, turn left at a white metal fence up Sandy Lane.

Turn left at the end of Sandy Lane and along the un-signed lane. At the end of this, there is a crossroads. Ride straight ahead towards the mock Tudor house. Carry on along Cassia Green Lane and take the first left up another lane, a narrow, bumpy but thankfully short ride.

On reaching the junction at the end of the lane, turn left, go along the road and down the hill towards Cassia Green. There is a telephone box on the right at the bottom of the hill. Go under a disused railway bridge and climb the hill until Salters Wall is reached.

Section e-a

Salters Wall is on the edge of Winsford. At the end of the road turn left. Ride down Chester Road and past a church on the right down towards Winsford Centre. On reaching the end of Delamere Street (a continuation of Chester Road), take the first exit off the roundabout, and ride down the A54.

Winsford Station is 2 miles away. On reaching the first set of traffic lights ride straight ahead. Carry on through the second set of light and once again follow the road ahead. The dual carriageway goes down hill until it reaches a roundabout. At this point, the railway is signposted. Take the third exit, follow the A54 back to the Station which is approximately a mile away from the roundabout.